SEIZE THE OPPORTUNITY OPEN THE CHAMPAGNE

A Collection of Inspiring Tales

Sujit Sengupta

© Sujit Sengupta 2021

All rights reserved

All rights reserved by author. No part of this publication may be reproduced, stored in a retrieval system or transmitted in any form or by any means, electronic, mechanical, photocopying, recording or otherwise, without the prior permission of the author.

Although every precaution has been taken to verify the accuracy of the information contained herein, the author and publisher assume no responsibility for any errors or omissions. No liability is assumed for damages that may result from the use of information contained within.

First Published in June 2021

ISBN: 978-93-5427-914-0

BLUEROSE PUBLISHERS

www.bluerosepublishers.com
info@bluerosepublishers.com
+91 8882 898 898

Illustrations: Maitrayee Majumder

Cover: Fayez Zameer

Typographic Design: Tanya Raj Upadhyay

Distributed by: BlueRose, Amazon, Flipkart

DEDICATED TO

Arina, Mihir and Samika, my precious grandchildren,

For them to know their 'Dadu'

Foreword

By Dr. Len Rogers

I have known Sujit Sengupta since he was a manager at Philips India, the conglomerate for whom I was a consultant for 15 years. Sujit was one of the executives selected for advanced management training and concentrating on sales and marketing. Sujit stood out as a highly productive achiever.

Were it not for his love of teaching, he would have achieved high office in Philips. In both his professional and academic work his diligence, application and accomplishment are impeccable.

He is highly skilled in team management and training and long experienced in marketing and sales, particularly in customer management. He continues to advance his knowledge and we remain in regular contact exchanging views on a variety of complex management and training activities, which in recent years have of necessity been extensively revised in the pandemic environment.

I have no hesitation in recommending *Seize the Opportunity, Open the Champagne* to all aspiring and seasoned sales and marketing managers who wish to expand their knowledge and skills.

(Dr. Len Rogers is a renowned Professor in leading International business schools. In 1968 he was retained by Philips Gloeilampenfabrieken NV, Eindhoven, to help Philips' executives to develop their potential and has directed the activities of several companies).

About the Author

Professor Sujit Sengupta has never stopped learning. Since starting his career in the early 70s in Consumer electronics as a management trainee, post his M. Tech from IIT Bombay, he has led a hectic and eventful career, the latter part of which has been spent in senior positions. Upon retirement, he reinvented himself and now teaches marketing and sales management at IILM Institute of Higher Education, imparting nuances of business and the science and art of it, building on ideas from his own experience as he had practiced in his corporate life. He has made learning a part of his life, putting extra value to what he imparts to the new generation of managers and students. This book is his first published work, borne out of his own experience at workplace.

Acknowledgements

It is not easy to pen down your thoughts when you set upon writing your first book. Many simple incidents have inspired me into writing – I remember how one day Shashi Sunny, a professionally qualified writer and a journalist friend described over a cup of coffee that she had embarked upon ghost writing and that how it was a completely unknown territory for her till then. I found her latest assignment quite exciting and thought of sharing some of my life's stories through a book myself. Thank you, Shashi, for kindling that first desire that later germinated through this book. I enjoyed those conversations during our tea-coffee *tête-à-tête* and received valuable tips that helped shape my book.

I thank my mentor Dr Len Rogers, former colleagues, friends, and well-wishers Ashis Sen, Atanu Ganguli, Debashish Paul, Gautam Sen, Oscar Braganza, Prakash Waknis, Punya Palit, Dr Tushar Roy and Upal Chakraborty for contributing bits of their own experience and sparing their valuable time for my book. Their contributions have undoubtedly enriched my book and have added an extra dimension to it. I also would like to thank Arun Gupta, Pawan Kapur and Yogesh Mathur for providing inputs to my stories; Rakesh Chaudhury and Rupak Chatterjee for their valuable suggestions. A special mention of author Ms Radhika Mitra's name should also be made here for helping me, sitting at the other side of the globe. I must also include the name of Mr Subir Adhikari – thanks to him, I gained the much-needed confidence to go ahead with this project.

I thank my family, especially my sons Anirban and Prasenjit, and daughters in law Shalini and Keka for having faith in my endeavour. I thank my wife Sumita for being the most stringent critic of my work and helping me develop the contents into a finished product.

Table of Contents

Introduction 1
Part One
CUSTOMER EXPERIENCE... 7
   1 One Champagne Bottle- Two Stories....................... 11
   2 The April Experience 17
   3 A Tale of Two Train Rides 20
   4 A Good IT System Can Be Dumb............................. 27
   5 Customer Experience - The Amazon Way 31
   6 Customer Experience: The Japanese Way 36
   7 One Small Thought Saves Many Pitfall 40
   8 Even Good Airlines are Street Smart 44
   9 Loyalty Regained 50

Part Two
LEADERSHIP... 53
   10 Leadership in Uncertain Times 57
   11 Trust Your Team, Be the Leader 60
   12 Nurture A Relationship Part I: Beauty Lies in The Eyes of The Beholder 65
   Nurture A Relationship Part II: The Gruesome Train Accident 69
   13 Inspire and Win 74
   14 His Fault, Their Fault, Not Mine 77
   15 Work First, Family Second 82
   16 When I Met Mr. Ratan Tata 85

17 Good Boys Also Win 90

18 From Football Field to Corporate Board Room 93

Part Three
SALES 101

19 Opportunity Doesn't Wait 106

20 The Pied Piper of Sadar Bazaar............................. 113

21 Think Strategy, Choose Change 118

22 What's So Special About Nordstrom 125

23 How Not to Sell!.. 131

24 The Magical Return on Investment 134

Part Four
MARKETING & BRANDING 137

25 Where A Distributor Becomes A Brand................. 140

26 A Peep into Rural India 143

27 Birth of A Brand.. 147

28 The Big Launch of a Small Car 153

Part Five
TECHNOLOGY IN BUSINESS 163

29 Think Design 167

30 Towards E-Commerce Strategy 172

31 Mid-Life Crisis in Tech Jobs................................. 179

Part Six
MY STORY 185

Education.. 186

Philips India Ltd. New Delhi 1969- 1980 187

Philips India Ltd. 1980 – 1986 188

Solidaire India, Chennai 1986- 1988........................ 189

Philips India Ltd. 1988- 1990 190
BPL Sanyo Utilities & Appliances 1990- 1994 190
National Panasonic India 1994- 1996 191
Usha International Ltd. 1996- 2007 192
IILM Institute of Higher Education, New Delhi, 2007-
2020 193
Contributors 195

some extra value to what I taught to the new generation. I believed in learning by doing instead of from textbooks and theories. This was my way of 'giving back to the community'. The process helped me get in touch with various non-profit organisations and business enterprises and conduct training workshops in different disciplines of management for their members and employees. Thus, unlike a full-fledged academic, the knowledge that I imparted to my students was primarily from what I learnt and practised during work.

For me, a career in academics started during the last three years of my life in the corporate sector when I received an assignment to teach executive MBA students at a professionally run management institute in Delhi, once every week in the evenings. While teaching there, I seldom referred to any textbook. My point of reference would always be some incidence from my own professional life. It dawned on me early that you could pack your student with theories, but the knowledge would be forgotten over the years. Whenever I met an old student, which would be rare, the student would tell me how he or she had been able to apply the management principles or concepts in the circumstances they were exposed to by recalling my stories. I realised nothing was better than teaching with examples from real life.

I find teaching is a fulfilling experience when my students remember what they got to learn from me.

My Motivation

On a Sunday afternoon in April 2019, I went to a lunch gathering hosted by one of my ex-Philips colleagues at a club in New Delhi. It was a gathering of about forty-five

Introduction

Tell me the facts and I'll learn. Tell me the truth and I will believe. But tell me a story and it will live in my heart forever.'

-An old Native American proverb

This book is all about stories, the incidents that took place in my work life during a long span of 37 years. These engaging stories imparts lessons in management practices in the fields of Customer Experience, Leadership, Sales, Marketing & Branding and Technology in Business.

My association with top multinational companies, Indian companies, and a home-grown family run business enabled me to go through a diverse work environment and culture. I could avail of opportunities for international travels, could nurture valuable relationships with a wide section of professionals through networking, and in the process absorbed lessons that were outside the scope of any business school.

Upon retirement, I was associated with IILM Institute of Higher Education, New Delhi for 13 long years, teaching the nuances of Business to young students. Narrating some of my life's experiences to these students or at workshops by way of examples of some management theories came naturally to me. It helped them comprehend the topic better as they could relate to real-life situations. I made learning a part of my life simultaneously, adding people. When I joined the party, the hostess was conducting a storytelling competition by way of a party game. A story had to be narrated by the guests with a time limit of 3 to 5 minutes. It was a perfect setting with a glass of white wine to relax and enjoy the afternoon.

One after another the guests narrated experiences ranging from spotting a ghost in a bungalow somewhere in Europe to getting chased by wild elephants in North Bengal. I was wondering which story to narrate when out of a spark somewhere in my mind I was reminded of the day when I had applied and appeared for an interview at Lal Bahadur Shastri Institute of Management in New Delhi. I was asked by the Director to narrate the happiest and saddest moments of my career. That afternoon, in front of my friends in the club I narrated that story – *One Champagne Bottle, Two Stories*.

I received the first prize. The seed for a book of 'storytelling' was planted that day.

Most of the good books on management that are available are written by international authors. The cases in these books relate to their situations and do not appropriately fit Indian work conditions many a time. Therefore, Indian students cannot fully relate to them. I have been on the lookout for a locally authored book that would provide access to Indian situations and case studies. And it is then that I realised that I have a stock of particularly good cases, and I could pen down some of them!

The Right Moment

Covid-19 brought in a pandemic in March 2020. It forced our Institute to adopt teaching online via Zoom platform and Work-From-Home.

This is when I began writing my stories, launched a website www.mamagmentmusing.com and uploaded them one by one. I received contributions from my colleagues and friends to enrich the website content. This book has taken shape from similar stories. One single thread that has joined most of the stories in this book is 'relationship management' based on trust. Customer relations, after-sales service, marketing, sales and even leadership all have a common element based on trust, contributing to a strong relationship bringing together the management and customers, thus bonding all the stakeholders in a successful enterprise.

At the end of each of my stories I have tried to focus on the management lessons that can be derived, and therefore, this book will be a useful handbook of incidents and situations for Indian middle management executives and aspiring managers. Out of respect to the departed souls, I have withheld some names of people mentioned in the stories. And of people whose names appear, due permission has been taken. Since I went down memory lane as I narrated the events, the timeline could be erroneous in places. It is bound to happen when recalling a life span of 37 years. Today's youngsters may find the work environment different as narrated in some stories based on my old experiences. However, they will appeal to them nonetheless because the narrations tell us how business was done at that time. The stories depict the pictures of corporate life in the seventies, through the eighties and nineties when life did not become digital, yet business used to be equally competitive. And as the disruptive digital platform changes business in the 2000s, when some of my stories are set, business insights remain the same. My effort has been to present vignettes from my work life and my insights on the pages of this book and if some young minds find them interesting, I will consider my effort worthwhile.

Part One

CUSTOMER EXPERIENCE

Dinesh Mohgaonkar and his wife Deepa were travelling Singapore Airlines economy class from Delhi to Singapore. When it was dinner time, the cabin crew looked at her chart and served both non-vegetarian meals. Dinesh requested a vegetarian meal for his wife Deepa. She reconfirmed and checked both had been marked as non-vegetarian. Since the tickets were booked by an agent, Dinesh was not sure whose mistake it was, and there was no spare vegetarian meal available. Deepa had to politely refuse her non-vegetarian meal. However, after serving everyone in the economy class, the cabin crew returned with a vegetarian meal that she was able to obtain from the business class section. Both Dinesh and Deepa were happy and thanked the cabin crew.

The story could have ended here. However, when dinner time was over, the cabin crew came back to their seat and asked them whether they would be returning to Delhi by the same airlines. Dinesh nodded and she said, 'Let me make a correction in my device so that on the return journey you are saved of this inconvenience'. On the return leg, Deepa got a vegetarian meal as desired. Dinesh had made a mental note: His first choice would always be Singapore Airlines.

Businesses understand the term 'Lifetime Value of a Customer', ie how much value it can return to the organisation over repeated visits. They also know if the customer does not like the experience, it does not matter what engineering, production, quality assurance, or anyone else inside the organisation says or believes. The customer defines quality and value and not organisations. EXPERIENCE is the heart of the Value Creation Process.

A delivery system is crucial in ensuring that all customers are provided with the experience that they expect.

A customer has multiple interactions with an organisation: before the purchase is made, during and post-sale. Large companies are usually organised into divisions and functions in product development, operations, sales, marketing, customer support and finance. Each division acts in self-interest and focuses on its own success –a fortress that protects its ideas and has its own leadership and culture. Yet, the organisation needs to think and act in terms of the entire customer experience and herein lies the challenge.

When customers share their story, they are not just sharing pain points. They teach how to make product, service, and business better. Loyal customers for life are created through improving service continuously and concentrating on service recovery.

Organisations need to nurture customer relationships, enhance trust, and positively reinforce engagements with customers.

When I teach young students getting ready to step into their professional life, I try to focus on the importance of Customer Experience as an essential part of Marketing. The youngsters studying management today are the future generation of entrepreneurs, professionals in the corporate world, manufacturers or they may be the future heads of some start-up industry. But everywhere they need to be conscious about their customer and care about the customer experience for the growth of their business establishments whether they deliver offline or online.

What does it mean to be customer-centric in this scenario?

In today's disruptive business, old methods do not prepare a CEO for what we see now and herein lies the leadership challenge casting him/ her into this new role - a customer centred company *builds relationships and value with customers beyond just product itself, makes plans and decisions keeping the impact of customers in mind.*

Developing a customer-oriented mindset amongst the employees provides the right culture even in today's context. Simply digitising does not ensure reliability and consistency. The world is getting more and more connected. Yet, a complete customer experience remains elusive for many.

1

One Champagne Bottle- Two Stories

One story is of happiness and one story is of sadness.

It was the Christmas Eve of 1972 in Delhi. Upon joining Philips India as a management trainee, my first posting after induction was as the Workshop Service In-charge of the two-story complex Philips Service Centre at 66, Janpath, New Delhi. This Regional Service Centre repaired all kinds of Philips equipment from Radios, Audio Systems, Television sets to Health Care Systems. We accepted international guarantee for Philips' equipment bought from the overseas markets. My expertise was in Television repairs and those days, only Black & White TV sets existed; we did not manufacture them in India back then. Final checking of the Television sets could only be done from 6 PM onwards with the start of the Doordarshan telecast and I invariably stayed back late. I was fresh out of college then and had sound knowledge of Electronics. I became quite adept in repairing other gadgets also. My job was to train and assist the technicians employed at the service centre as well as our dealers. Though the Service Centre timings were from 9.30 AM to 6 PM, for our customer timings was from 10 AM till 5.30 PM. In the interim period, the shutters were kept three quarters down. This half an hour extra in the evening enabled our technicians to close job sheets, receive the work allocation for the next day and for the cashier to tally the accounts of the money received from customers.

At 6.15 PM on that pre- Christmas evening, our security guard came up to me and said that two foreigners were insisting upon being allowed to enter the Service Centre to get their Audio Cassette Recorder repaired. They had purchased it from the Netherlands and getting it repaired was urgent. No amount of explanation from the security guard that the office was closed for customers and everybody had left could convince the two of them. They wanted to meet someone from the office - preferably a senior. I walked down the staircase and to the parking lot where these two foreigners were waiting, holding the Philips equipment. Before I could tell them that we were closed for the day, the foreigners, who were Russians, made an earnest appeal that the Philips cassette recorder was only 3 weeks old and suddenly went 'dead'. They had lined up a Christmas eve programme at the Embassy that evening, and a party could not possibly start without music. I pleaded that except for me and another colleague who had also specialised in TV repairs, all others had left. They would not move and kept on repeating *pozhaluista* (Russian for 'please'). When they did not get convinced, I said, 'I will personally try with my limited knowledge, and if lucky…good, otherwise…'. They thanked me sensing a ray of hope while I carried the equipment upstairs for an inspection.

The equipment was an audio player manufactured at Philips Netherland – their most popular model N2400, introduced that year. The product had very superior sound quality. Many 'Desis' returning from the overseas had one tucked under their arms. The recorder suffered from a very common complaint in India. Wide voltage fluctuations that prevailed those days made the imported apparatus vulnerable and as a result rendered them 'dead'. The solution we had discovered locally was to replace the 'thermal fuse' with a somewhat higher rating. I anticipated this and the Eureka moment arrived. After replacing the fuse that took me barely 10 minutes, the recorder came alive!

I told the security guard to inform the two gentlemen waiting outside. They stepped into the reception and I played for them a demonstration tape. It sounded great. Thrilled beyond imagination, they said, '*Spasiba Spasiba*' (thank you, thank you) in Russian. and asked for the repair bill. I told them not to worry, the equipment was on international guaranteed terms and it would be free of charge. The joy and satisfaction reflecting on their faces had to be seen to be believed. I climbed upstairs to resume my work. A few moments later the security guard came up once again and said, 'Sir, they want to see you once more.'

What could have happened?

The guard replied, 'They are asking for you.' I went downstairs and walked to the car park. With a big smile on his face, one of the Russians said, 'Enjoy your Christmas,' and gifted me a bottle of Champagne.

This was one of the happiest moments of my career. However, it was not the end of the story.

My happiness did not last long.

I did not carry home the bottle. Instead, kept it in the office for my colleagues to see and share my happiness the next day. In the morning when my boss arrived, I narrated the story and showed him the Champagne bottle. After listening to me patiently, and giving a pat on my back, he took the bottle in his hand and said 'Thank you very much…'

My heart missed a beat – this was one of the most unhappy moments of my life.

Key Learning:

'Service means satisfying customers, and when we satisfy our customers, we, in turn, find satisfaction in a job well

done. Satisfied customers and satisfied employees - that is what constitutes true service'. – said Konosuke Matsushita, the founder who created the vast business empire National Panasonic. I had worked for its Indian subsidiary from 1994-96, but much before that, in fact, at the very beginning of my career, I experienced that the little things when done right could mean so much to someone that it could make a big difference in life. In this story, the customer's happiness is reflected all around him, touching the service provider's heart in the process. The job as a service provider is not limited to just acting in case of a complaint. A service provider must have an inner passion to go beyond the given outline of his job profile and try and help a customer to the best of his ability. Greeting customers with sincere kindness instead of obligated kindness helps in building customer relationships.

Vignettes from My Diary

Citing an example of going out of the way to help experienced as recent as March 2021, I had read that Apple stores employees are not allowed to say 'no' directly. They would have to say something like, 'Yes, I absolutely can help you and I'd love to.' I upgraded my iPhone 6 to iPhone 6-S in October 2020. The Bluetooth of the new phone was not pairing with my Honda Amaze car audio system. The old iPhone 6 had no problems and there was no urgency in getting it checked due to Covid-19 at that time. I drove to the new Apple store close by my residence. The technical representative tried adjusting the phone settings at the store and wanted it to be checked in the car. He walked with me to the parking lot, a small distance away and checked on my iPhone. As it was not working, he rechecked on his iPhone. It was not pairing either. In these circumstances, the standard response would be to direct the customer to Honda Motors as the fault was not with the iPhone device. He clicked a picture of the car audio front panel and forwarded it to a contact via WhatsApp at Honda. He was guided through a few simple steps in the settings and the Bluetooth paired!

2

The April Experience

I get up to an unusually quiet April morning. The balmy dawn with chirping birds, clean, almost a pristine atmosphere reminds me of the Aprils of my childhood. But we are far removed in reality – it is the April of 2020, the early days of a pandemic and ensuing a nationwide lockdown.

Every year it is this month when we look forward to our Bengali *Nabobarsho* celebrations, to the wedding anniversary of the elder son and the birthday of our youngest grandchild in London. We were to travel overseas in March 2020 for these two celebrations followed by the birthday of our grandson in May in California. The flights got cancelled. We were bracing ourselves for an unknown pandemic until the elder daughter-in-law found a way to make the most of this situation. She planned a virtual family get together on-line across three continents, where the child cut her third birthday cake. She also wanted us to enjoy a five-star meal home-delivered, which proved to be more difficult than the online party as no five-star or equivalent restaurant from her list of numbers was offering home delivery. Until she contacted Marriott hotel from her collection of hotel phone numbers.

The number belonged to JW Marriott, Kolkata. We live in Delhi, but Marriott Kolkata sent her their online menu without a fuss and with the help of the link sent by them, she ordered a spread for us.

We received a message from her that food would be delivered on the desired day between 12 noon and 1 in the afternoon. The hospitality industry thrives on a positive experience, but how Marriott Kolkata responded and coordinated with their Delhi hotel in delivering the perfect meal was amazing. JW Marriott, Delhi Aero city was the place from where our delivery came, and we became aware of it only when we received a message asking for our feedback and our source of receiving the menu. One phone call to a hotel in Kolkata, more than 1000km away from Delhi, and a seamless process took care of timely delivery. Mr Karan Dhaliwal from JW Marriott Aero city, Delhi wrote politely that this bit of information would help the chain move forward. It surely would. Living in South Delhi, I was impressed. This hotel near the Delhi airport not only delivered warm food but also honoured the scheduled time. And it took care to touch base with the customer too. This consistency in service of an already established brand is what makes a happy customer experience.

Key Learning:

Pulido, Stone & Strevel wrote in an article in McKinsey March 2014 that the 3 Cs of customer satisfaction were Consistency, Consistency, Consistency. It is not enough to make customers happy with each individual interaction. Companies that perfect customer journeys reap enormous rewards including enhanced customer and employee satisfaction, reduced churns, increased revenues, and lowered costs.

The year 2020 will surely go down the world history for Covid 19, a highly contagious virus that plays havoc with human lives and livelihood. This April incident, in the background of a nationwide lockdown, sums up how important consistency is in customer service.

3

A Tale of Two Train Rides

Popularised by pioneering and successful retailer Harry Gordon, founder of Selfridge Departmental Store in London, 'The customer is always right' is a motto or slogan which exhorts service staff to give a high priority to customer satisfaction.

Well, not always. Like all other human beings, the customer can be wrong too……. right? But how can be the situation turned into a win-win case when the customer is wrong?

We got the answer from our own experience. In the summer of 2012, my wife and I as customers went horribly wrong. The circumstances did not need to go so horribly wrong if the person who dealt with us was more sensitive, and discerning, as every one of us ought to be at our individual workplace so that the experience ended as a happy one.

It was a mistake committed by me while booking a railway ticket online some days prior to our journey. Let me give you the details first: We wished to visit the Golden Temple at Amritsar and booked two tickets in the Executive Class by the early morning Shatabdi that ran daily from New Delhi to Amritsar. The COVID-19 pandemic was nowhere on the horizon then. Since we had to attend to some urgent business in Ludhiana the next morning, I also booked two tickets for our trip from Amritsar to Ludhiana the same day again by Shatabdi that left Amritsar around five in the evening. It was going to be a pleasure cum work trip, and I found that the timing of the Shatabdi trains was exactly right for paying our obeisance to the Granth Sahib at the Golden Temple at a leisurely pace and have a good night's rest at a Ludhiana hotel before concentrating on the work in hand the next day. The morning trip to Amritsar was uneventful, though I found travelling by Executive Class in a Shatabdi did not make any sense anymore – in fact, it was a waste of money. The Railways, having worked on an excellent concept with its Shatabdi services decades ago did not bother to maintain the coaches or upkeep the services any longer, at least till 2012 – a sure case of complacency arising from monopoly in business. A few lodged complaints in the designated complaint book.

The rest of the day went off nicely. The temple complex helped instil calmness and serenity in us. We felt blessed. A stroll inside the age-old Jallianwala Bagh stirred emotions in us – we witnessed the inhumanity of the British ruling class as we had read in our textbooks. With a mixed feeling we went for a very satisfying lunch at `Bharawan da Dhaba`, and then we proceeded towards the railway station, and upon spotting the Shatabdi waiting on the platform, boarded the train. The journey to Ludhiana too appeared to be uneventful, at least so we thought.

Things did not remain hunky-dory for long. The ticket checker came into our compartment and approached us. Most of the seats this time round were unoccupied, and we recognised the uniformed ticket checker – he was the same guy who was there during our onward journey to Amritsar. However, one look at our tickets and he said in Hindi, *'Aapka booking to morning train ki hain.'* (You booked your tickets for the morning train). Perplexed, I took back the computer prints and looked at them myself, and before I could fathom what was wrong with them, he said again, *'Paanch paanch ka Shatabdi ke liye hain yeh, jo aaj saberey Amritsar se start hui thi.'* (Your ticket is for the five minutes past five o'clock Shatabdi, and it had left Amritsar station today morning.)

It took some time to sink in, but I realised my mistake. While applying for a reservation online, I had chosen the 05:05 train instead of the 17:05 one. There was another Shatabdi leaving Amritsar for New Delhi in the morning as well. I nodded in admission, and before I could utter any word, he said, *'Aap dono isi train mein Dilli se Amritsar aye the aaj, toh subeh train miss honey ka koi sawal hi nahin hain, lekin mere liye toh aap abhi without ticket travel kar rahein hain, hain na?'* (I can see it is a genuine mistake on your part as you two were in the morning Shatabdi from Delhi today and it's not a case of missing the morning Shatabdi from Amritsar and travelling by the evening one instead. It's not intentional, but as far as I'm concerned you are caught travelling without a valid ticket, isn't it?)

I offered to buy a fresh set of Amritsar-Ludhiana tickets, and requested him not to charge any penalty – after all, he knew that we were not trying to cheat. But he said that we had to pay double the actual Amritsar – Delhi fare by Executive Class as per the rules. There was not going to be any concession for our getting down at Ludhiana – we were ticket-less travellers according to the law. Well, the rule book and the law were on his side. And he did not budge from his argument. As I realised that he was in no mood to show us any concession, I tried to coax and cajole. 'I know you have a proper rule book, but surely you could use your discretion and help me out,' I said. 'Why don't you just charge me ordinary chair car fare for two from Amritsar to Ludhiana? That way you do not break any rule, and I will not be penalized like a criminal – you know I did buy the tickets and wasn't trying to cheat the railways. It was an oversight!'

He didn't argue anymore and came to the point straight – *'Aap dhai hazar rupaye penalty ke samet de doh aur chair car ka ticket banalo.'* (Give me Rs.2500/- for chair car ticket with penalty) 'That's the rule,' he smugly said. Again, it took some time for me to comprehend fully what he was asking me to do. 'Will you give me a receipt?' I asked him. He simply looked at me. *'Achha thik he aap Rs.1000/- de deejiye,'* (Ok give me Rs.1000/-) and walked away leaving me in a state of quandary.

Either you pay a bribe or be a law-abiding citizen and pay heavily for a mistake that had been committed inadvertently.

I remember a similar experience that I had while travelling from London to Norwich in Northern England by train. Following my son's advice, we started from home one hour in advance as traffic jams were quite common on London roads and reached the station quite early without facing any congestion on our way. After some time, we heard an announcement that the Norwich bound train was waiting at a certain platform. We located the platform and boarded the coach whose number was mentioned in our ticket. However, we did not check our wristwatches, nor did we confirm the waiting train's timing of departure at the information counter. We had boarded an earlier train than the one in which our tickets were booked.

As the ticket checker approached us and we handed over the tickets after our train had covered quite a bit of distance, our mistake was brought to our notice by the checker. We looked at him helplessly – we were not only in a foreign country where the colour of our skin was always a suspect, but we were also at a disadvantage if we had to pay a penalty, considering the exchange value of the rupee in terms of pound sterling. But the fair-skinned British employee said nonchalantly, 'Don't commit the same mistake on your way back,' (Ours was a two-way ticket) and went about his job without a fuss. Didn't the British have rule books? Of course, they did, but their employees also had their mind and common sense which they applied to address situations in the right way.

As scams, grafts and bribery take the centre stage of our public life, I realise what ails our society. It is lack of training of our human resources. If the ticket checker back home had accepted my suggestion of issuing a fresh set of Amritsar Ludhiana tickets by chair car, the railways would not have been a loser – I had already paid for the Amritsar–Ludhiana trip, and this I was paying extra by way of a penalty for my mistake. Moreover, he had already accepted that we were not trying to con the railways. In this situation, my problem would have been alleviated by paying less. Bribery is commonly nurtured in Government and public sector organisations that have a monopoly in certain businesses. Citizens, paying for the services are not treated as customers to be served, but as sitting ducks to be exploited.

Key Learning:

The situation in this story could have been the ideal win-win for the service provider and the customer. After all, good service is when your customer feels he is right, or he is not wronged, even when the rule book says he is. It is worth quoting Richard Branson, the founder of Virgin Group that runs Virgin Atlantic amongst other service providing enterprises. He wrote in a syndicated article,

'.... staffers should treat the rules more as flexible guidelines, to be followed as the situation demands. The customer is not always right, and neither is the rule book.' According to him, a well-documented rule book is a must when cash and accounting are at issue. At the same time, he has acknowledged, *'Sometimes rules really are made to be broken.'* In the service industry, how far one can go to please a client is always a question as there is a risk of compromising one's business. Branson's answer is simple: empower the staff to use their common sense when handling questions and problems. *'Resolving problems this way has multiple benefits for both the customer and the company,'* he says.

4

A Good IT System Can Be Dumb

I had been ordering medicines from an online pharmacy since 2018. It offered a good discount on a certain day of the week then and promised to deliver the medicines, all carefully and meticulously packed, in one day.

I received the following message within the promised time: 'Hi, your ****shipment with AWB No ***** is out for delivery and will be delivered today.'

It was simply a perfect service without any scope for any complaint. However, the satisfaction level changed drastically when I received the next message – Hi, we missed delivering your **** shipment AWB ***** today as consigned not available / consignee not responding. If incorrect, call…or email…

I did see a missed call on my mobile number, which I had failed to answer for reasons of connectivity or something else, but nobody had come to deliver the packet to me at my delivery address where I had been present all along. I had to complain, and the packet arrived after 3 days. I have had the same experience whenever I missed a delivery boy's call, even if there were people to receive the packet. Why did they fail to provide delivery at the address?

This is where a perfect customer experience went awry. The word customer experience is required to be understood in two parts – customer (+) experience. In this case, the online pharmacy had adopted a good IT system but the organisation, in the eyes of the customer, was not ready with good work culture, despite my telling them several times that I would rather have the consignment delivered at the given address and not be contacted only by phone calls. As far as I was concerned, the delivery boy was not at the given address to deliver the consignment! The online pharmacy probably had outsourced the delivery. A good IT system can be dumb in this respect. Culture drives the behaviour of people irrespective of what is written in the strategy document. If the culture does not support the ability and efficiency of the system, it is doomed to fail, a fool proof IT system cannot salvage its reputation.

Delivering an amazing customer experience requires the application of 3 'R's and the 1 'C'. First 'R', Relevance, is offering the customer what is needed and when it is needed. The second, 'Reliability', is timeliness, but the more important factor is the 'C' here, which is 'Consistency'. Organisations adopt IT systems to deliver consistency. Delivery is dependent upon the culture in the organisation and consistency is where culture and systems connect. IT only acts as an enabler; it does not deliver experience by itself.

The third 'R', which I am deliberately listing at the end is the organisation's ability to be 'Responsive' – it is the ability to listen with the intent to understand and with a view to act. In the case of the above-mentioned online pharmacy, when I told them to come to the given address and ring the doorbell, they failed to act accordingly. Most people listen with the intent to only reply. When consumers are unhappy about something and express dissatisfaction, the response generally is 'we are listening to you. Give us the details and let us see how we can help you.' This is not being responsive; it is reputation management.

Experiences are a mixed bag. While customers are quick to acknowledge quality products and services, they go to greater lengths to amplify bad experiences. Let us face it: today, many customer experiences can be disastrous.

Key Learning:

'Culture eats Strategy for breakfast...' says management guru Peter Drucker and the lack of it is felt in every field. Organisational work culture must flow from the top, and employees at the front line will imbibe it through training, motivation, and discipline.

As the Covid-19 settles down, tech companies will be in a hiring frenzy to take advantage of a world shifting increasingly to being digital. The millennial generation is looking for an experience everywhere even in a crisis rather than buying products, and as they edge out the GenX at workplaces, customer experience is bound to evolve faster.

Vignettes from My Diary

My friend Raghuvansh bought a branded twin-blade shaving system of a reputed company from a dealer in South East Delhi. While opening the pack he found that the outer pack and the razor were broken, and he mailed with all the details attaching a picture of the outer packaging to the company on September 5, 2016. Three days later a lady phoned him to say that someone would visit his residence in the next 7-10 days to replace the defective razor. After waiting for 15 days when no one showed up, he sent reminders of inaction asking at what age was the company living. On October 7, the Consumer Care Team informed Raghuvansh that they had dispatched the product. However, the tracking details were not available with them yet and no sooner it was received my friend would be updated. Subsequent silence prompted Raghuvansh to write for the last time. Finally, on November 18, Customer Care apologised for the delay and sent Big Bazaar vouchers of INR100/- and assured him again that as they received the tracking details he would be contacted. Raghuvansh never received the replacement shaving system as promised, nor did he visit Big Bazaar to redeem the coupon.

5

Customer Experience - The Amazon Way

Once, on a visit to Mountain View in California, I bought an Amazon Fire Stick from Best Buy. The plug-in and play device provided access to popular apps such as Netflix, YouTube, Hotstar, Prime Video, Voot, Sony TV etc. The television set needed to be connected to a Wi-Fi network only. As I purchased it in the U.S, the operating voltage was 110 V.

After a week of my return to India, it was plugged into the TV with an adapter (110V/ 220V). The screen was blank. My presumption was that the device needed adjustments for India and that it would need an intervention by customer care. Unfortunately, I was not able to locate a service arrangement where I could seek help. I dialled Amazon's 24-hr helpline number (1800 3000 9009) from my Airtel network, got connected without any hitch and within 3 rings a customer service representative responded to my call. The call was picked up at Amazon, Seattle office. I briefly narrated details of my purchase and the difficulty I was facing in installing it. I was asked to provide the serial no of the device. He said that the Fire Stick needed to be re-configured as I was based in India and he would put me through to the right section that handled it. However, just before he finished, the call got abruptly disconnected. Our conversation lasted just 20 secs.

As I was preparing to call back, my phone rang with a calling number that had +353 prefixed. As the dial area code revealed, it was an Amazon helpline based in Dublin (Ireland). Continuing from where the Seattle person left the conversation, the Dublin service representative went on to provide me further advice and guidance, but midway the call got disconnected once more. This brief conversation was of no help.

After a while, my phone rang once more. I could identify from the dialling code – it was Amazon, Chennai and the service representative was of good help giving me step-by-step instructions on the installation process when suddenly the call snapped. This call had lasted 60 secs. My frustration with the mobile network was annoying.

Within moments, another call originating from Dublin took me through the next step from where the Chennai representative got interrupted, and he had hardly spoken for 15 secs when the call snapped again. The final call that followed in a minute from London and continuing from where the Dublin representative had stalled kept me engaged for about 150 secs taking me through the final installation process, this time uninterruptedly, and helped sign onto the Wi-Fi network. What was most amazing about the whole process was its seamless operation. How the next individual was able to start the conversation from where the previous one left – every event happening in real time – was nothing short of a wonder. Perhaps the unfinished conversation with the client was visible on screen!

In contrast, the same year while booking the tickets to the U.S with a top online travel company here in Delhi, by oversight I forgot to mention the Frequent Flyer No. (FFN) that would have enabled me to earn extra miles. I phoned their call centre and the following was the conversation that followed:

> 1. Thanks for calling... How can I help you?
>
> 2. Please identify your registered mobile no and address.

After proving the details, the answers that followed was:

> 3. Sorry, Sir, this query is not handled by us, I am directing you to the appropriate section that deals with it. Meanwhile thanks for calling...and we appreciate your patience. How else can I help you?

The call got redirected and recorded music played continuously as I waited. After a while, another operator surfaced and repeated processes (1) to (3).

When I guessed I got to the right customer service executive, the automated voice recording announced, 'All our service representatives are busy; your call is important to us, kindly stay online.' After keeping the receiver glued to my ears for 12 min, the call got disconnected.

I called again; the second experience was a replication of the first. In frustration, I hung up.

At the airport, while checking in, I requested the airline's staff to endorse my frequent flier no.

Before the commencement of my return journey from the U.S, to be doubly sure that the staff at the check-in counter had endorsed the FFN, I dialled the online travel company's call centre from the U.S. The experience was no different. On top of that, the international call cost me a good amount. Finally, I had to seek help from one of my ex-students, an employee of the travel company for confirmation of my request.

The two contrasting experiences pointed towards the company's responsiveness and culture. The Amazon experience created a sense of positivity in a customer. The customer develops an attachment and loyalty to the brand. The second incident makes the customer choose another supplier at the best available opportunity.

Key Learning:

Customers expect more natural communications from brands today. Marketers, therefore, have the challenge of creating a personal connection with the increasing use of automation. Companies now expect to compete mostly on customer experience, and this is bound to evolve faster.

In his book 'Everything Store and the Age of Amazon' Jeff Bezos describes that his only focus area was Customer and he often worked backwards to provide a unique Customer Experience. He tracked two important metrics – average talk time (the average time an employee spent on the phone with the customer) and contacts per order (the no. of times a purchase necessitated a customer phone call or e-mail).

Vignettes from My Diary

My car insurance was due for renewal. I received a renewal notice from the insurance service provider and the policy was renewed. On April 20, 2019, I received the following mail:

'We would like to take this opportunity to thank you for choosing XXX Company. We are fully committed to providing insurance products and services in a convenient and satisfying manner. Please find attached your Policy document'.

On May 2, 2019, I received another mail from the same insurance provider that only 3 days remained to renew the policy!!! Clearly, it was a case of one company with multiple databases. What was needed was a single source of clean and consolidated data to do Customer Relationship Management well.

6

Customer Experience: The Japanese Way

The experience I gained working with Japanese and European companies have been vastly different. Though I first visited Japan in 2018, much later than working with National Panasonic India between the years 1994-96, my constant interaction with Japanese colleagues helped me gather knowledge about their working methods. To most Japanese people, work preceded any other priorities in life; their family came second. A Japanese husband's esteem in the eyes of their spouse was gauged by how late he arrived home from work. A consensus management style, procedure and systems-driven, an abundant empathy towards customers, getting into meticulous details of every operation, a value for everyone's time and a continuous effort towards improvement have been the hallmark of their success.

In the summer of 2018, I decided to take a 3-day stopover at Tokyo with my wife on my way to San Francisco. My son had already made an extensive tour of this island nation and had been absolutely smitten by this country. Apart from it being a beautiful country worth a visit, I also wanted to confirm my views about Japan formed during my association with the Japanese companies. I also wanted to check what made this amazing country emerge out of destruction after the war and constantly face the threat of natural calamities. The grit and perseverance of the Japanese people never ceased to impress me. At every step of my interaction with people or process, I observed, took pictures, talked to people, and scribbled notes. It is difficult to build a comprehensive story during such a short stay, but positive management principles can be captured by linking to the background information I had possessed about this country. Here are a few experiences that attracted my attention:

1. When the Japanese are asked to explain something or present data, they tend to use visual means such as pictures, charts, diagrams, sketches, or graphs. The tourist guide, during our travel, invariably tried to explain instructions through pre-drawn sketches. In restaurants, the menu was displayed in the pictorial form at the entrance making it compelling and easily understandable. In contrast, when we are asked to elaborate on something, we tend to just use more words. When it is oral, it means we may go on and on talking, and if it is on paper that might mean a long string of paragraphs. This tends to be frustrating to a Japanese – and frustrating to us when we discover that they have not absorbed anything.

2. Most Japanese men and women wear solid colour suits (mostly black) and a white shirt to work. They maintain three sets of such suits. One set is given to the laundry each week; the other two sets are rotated during the week. This avoids spending wasteful time and resources in determining what to wear each day.

3. Japan has a severe crunch for space. I recall, once I had invited a Japanese colleague for dinner to our house in

Delhi and the first remark that he made was that their entire flat was the size of our living room! Consequently, in Japan, most hotels rooms are small and so are the toilets. Not more than one suitcase can be carried inside a room, otherwise, it would obstruct movement space. At times, the hotel lobby can be on a different floor. Labour is an expensive commodity like it is in every developed country, so no bell boys are generally available. If a guest arrives with multiple items of baggage, the extra bags are stored in the 'left luggage' room. The hotel allows the guest to keep it along with the trolley so that while checking out one has only to cart the trolley out and hail a coach or a taxi to the destination. This avoids the physical lifting of the luggage by the hotel customer.

4. Reverting to hotel rooms, after a hot shower, the mirrors inside the cubicle tend to get frosty (especially if washrooms are small) making it hard to view one's face. This happens with most hotels that I have stayed in.

Japanese hotels have a heating device mounted behind the mirror that helps in keeping a rectangular area of appx 2'x2' in the large mirror clear of frosting. This trend, though, is catching up now outside Japan.

5. The international Tokyo Narita airport handles around 50 per cent of international passengers' traffic in Japan and the check-in process is automated. The height of the baggage conveyor belt has been designed with the thought that passengers do not have to lift the baggage while placing it on the conveyor belt.

7. Immigration and customs at Narita are smooth and rapid with the least amount of waiting and walking. Consequently, passengers are not tired, which leaves them with sufficient time for thoughtful shopping. This results in the footfalls to duty-free shops high with a good rate of conversion.

Key Learning:

The Japanese indeed care about getting meticulous details to enhance customer experience. Caring about a customer does not have to be an expensive endeavour – it just requires creating moments of delight. Those moments, whether a larger gesture or something even as small as responding to customer inquiries within an hour on Twitter, stem from a promise. Adopting practices that elevate the customer experience undoubtedly produces a return on investment and provides a steady foundation upon which a brand can continue to grow. Great customer experience design is about injecting purpose and empathy into everything we do. And the Japanese do it very well.

7

One Small Thought Saves Many Pitfall

Cruises are fun. Cruises are de-stressing. One can literally let one's hair loose while onboard a cruise liner, as one can get to visit many new places without the hassles of packing, unpacking, and checking into new hotels during travel. Cruises are full of entertainment and also offer a great learning experience as any kind of travel to any new place does.

One can go on and on about the virtues of cruises. But a lesson in management practice? Well, much to our surprise, we found out that our travel to the Baltic Sea in mid-2013 would offer a quite different kind of experience. No, it was not that we met a Management Guru on our cruise liner. It was an altogether new kind of customer service offered by the cruise liner.

Anybody who has ever taken a cruise would know that you must leave your luggage at the check-in point at the port, much like one does at the airport check-in counter, keeping only a small carry-on bag if one wants to. Your key to your cabin and a multi-purpose Sea-Pass card is handed over to you. Your luggage is delivered outside your cabin, and since there can be more than a couple of thousands of tourists, depending on the size of the liner, delivering luggage can take quite a long time, sometimes stretching till the ship starts sailing in the evening.

This time around, we were in for a shock. Our suitcase did not arrive outside our room within the stipulated time, and we panicked – our ship was already on its journey to the next port. It is not an ideal situation where you are left with only your passport and credit card, and nothing else!

Upon enquiry, we were told to contact the reception and then we were guided to the security section of the ship. We were surprised and wondered what prohibited item we were carrying that even an international flight could not stop! Anyway, sure enough, we found our suitcase in a large room full of bags and suitcases and people scurrying around to locate their own stuff. There was a sticker pasted on our suitcase that read, 'Knife' in large letters! We were taken aback. International flights as well as our domestic ones allow knife in checked-in luggage. Besides, we were not carrying any knife! Then, suddenly we remembered –

there was a tiny Swiss-knife set in our suitcase and without saying much we rummaged through our belongings and took it out. 'You have to deposit the knife here,' said the very polite Security Officer to us, 'and you get it back when you leave the ship at the end of the whole trip.' She sounded very matter of fact, even as the thought of losing our small yet very handy knife crossed our mind – there was already a pile of many such items on her table, and there were many more suitcases still lying to be claimed by the owners. She asked for my Sea-Pass card and swiped it in the machine in front of her. The Sea-Pass card was a smart card with all the details of my identity (even the passports were handed over to the authorities at the check-in point). She signed on a piece of paper, put a stamp, and gave it to me. 'You claim your knife with this at the time of checking out,' she said.

Ours was a seven-night trip sailing to the Baltic from Copenhagen, with stopovers in Tallinn, St. Petersburg, Helsinki, and Stockholm, finally docking back at Copenhagen. The scenic beauty of European landscapes and seascapes, quaint old churches, the exotic marketplaces, different people with their exotic food, and above all, the magnificence of the erstwhile Tsars' life in St. Petersburg kept us overwhelmed all these days. The entertainment and shows onboard our ship, and the lavish spread at mealtime took the centre stage of our lives for the next few days. Our tiny old Swiss knife was the last thing on our mind.

Finally, on the eighth day, as we were ready to vacate our ship, we were as complacent as anybody would be after a happy time during a holiday. We were standing in two lines as one by one all of us were coming out of the ship after swiping our Sea-Pass card and getting back our passports. When it was my turn, I handed over the card to the security officer at the gate to swipe, and the machine sounded a loud blip, an alarm sounded and I was startled, and, panicked again. What went wrong? I was using this card regularly during all my trips onshore, then, what could indeed go wrong?

'Would you mind stepping this way, Sir?' I heard a polite voice saying a little away from the gate. I was scared but confident. I had not done anything wrong. I had not picked up anything from the ship wrongfully and carrying it with me. I followed the Security Officer to another desk. The officer swiped my card once more and said to me, 'You have to pick up your knife Sir. Can I have the deposit slip?'

Key Learning:

This story is a brilliant example of what in management parlance is called the Service Recovery process that is a critical – yet all too often missing – element in providing customer service that will attract and retain customers and have a positive impact on the bottom line of any business, no matter where it is located or what product or service it provides. The cruise liner must have experienced in the past that many tourists invariably forget to collect their items that are deposited at the time of checking in, the way we did, and later ask for its return. The cruise liner not only have to spend time and resources handling these 'unclaimed' belongings, but it also has to later trace the item and courier it to an unhappy customer. So, the 'smart card' is made smarter, and the tourist feels secured and happy!

8

Even Good Airlines are Street Smart

All the airlines must be looking after their upper-class passengers with equal attention and care. After all, airlines make money only on business fares. My experience as a business class passenger has been very ordinary, aside from the regular advantage and facilities over economy class. The attention of the ground staff, flight crew or even customer care turned out to be quite run of the mill. Was it discrimination because of our skin or should they care about the volume of dollars brought to the airlines? Airlines need to learn not every person who does not want to argue and does not want to show unhappiness can be treated casually and empathy is a great virtue in customer service.

My wife and I visit our sons, who have settled abroad, quite regularly. In 2017 when we planned our visit to London, our son sent us two business class return tickets – the name of the airline is withheld here. As senior citizens, he wanted us to travel in comfort and have an experience of flying business class. The flight from Delhi to London was indeed a memorable experience for both of us especially for my wife who was recovering from a bout of Chikungunya at that time. For the first time in many years, we did not have to wait in long queues during the security clearance and the check-in process. Apart from priority boarding, the service in the waiting lounge was courteous and we could help ourselves with champagne and cheese.

Once inside the aircraft, the upper-class seats were convertible into beds and tasty meals served on board - the flight was comfortable and enjoyable.

The evening return flight a month later, however, was an altogether different experience. The check-in process, followed by the world-class lounge at Heathrow International Airport was very impressive. But our happiness was short-lived as we were stopped at the boarding gate suddenly and asked to wait. Minutes ticked by and boarding was almost over. We started getting nervous. A priority boarding had gone horribly wrong for us two. Just as when boarding was to be completed, a young man in uniform addressed me, 'Sir, I am sorry to inform you that the electric mechanism of your seat is not working. Your seat will not recline and convert into a bed.'

By then we had become so anxious and were feeling so harassed that I suggested spontaneously, 'You can reassign me another seat, I am willing to move.' But the airline already had a devious plan.

'We are completely full Sir. If you agree to fly, we will compensate you with Euro 50 and credit 40,000 miles into your frequent flyer account'. We were Jet Privilege member and the thought of 40,000 miles delighted me momentarily – it was equivalent to two Delhi-Kolkata return journey tickets- a trip that I frequently made. A little discomfort during the 8-hour long night-time flight was worth its value, I thought, and I already started planning to pass time by watching movies with a wine glass in hand. My wife, however, cautioned me saying that she did not think the offer was good enough. But I was ready to slog it out one night to come back home. The airline's staff rather rudely said that it was all he could offer and did not discuss the matter any further.

Once onboard, my complacency started waning slowly. For, not only the bed, but the tray table was dysfunctional too and I was not able to watch any movie. I had to sip my drink and eat my dinner putting the plate on my lap. I had also to ask the attendant several times to hand over Euro 50 which was promised to me. Finally, the attendant declared, 'Sir, we cannot give you cash. Instead, you select a product from our duty-free catalogue worth the amount please.' This was the final shock. Controlling my anger, I quietly ordered a Diesel Eau de Toilette perfume. This too was handed over to me early in the morning a little while before landing was announced and after I issued the third reminder. I spent the entire 8-hour long flight sitting up in the business class section, dozing off uncomfortably, while my fellow travellers were nicely tucked in their comfortable seats. I felt cheated and taken for a ride by the airline, though it was largely due to my own foolishness. I could always refuse to fly unless the seat was fully functional!

Further disappointment was to follow. Even after two weeks of reaching Delhi, the promised 40,000 miles had not been credited to my Jet Privilege account. I felt it was time to retaliate. I complained to the airline's Customer Relations describing how the airline's staff took me for a ride.

Responding with the usual apologetic note, the airline insisted it was against their policy to credit the miles to a partner account and a credit of 50,000 miles which was equivalent to a one-way upper-class ticket of London to Delhi could only be credited to the airline's Frequent Flyer program. The 'like for like' offer notwithstanding, the hardships I had undergone was not acceptable; secondly to avail of this offer, I would need to buy another business class ticket for my wife when we travel next and thirdly, I was not bound to any airlines and whenever we travelled, we looked around for the best available fares.

I wrote back saying that as a reputed airline, I expected a better understanding of my situation and requested a credit of miles equivalent to two one-way premier economy tickets for both of us by the same airline which were 70,000 miles. I had boarded the flight, though I was under no obligation to travel that evening and had we chosen not to fly, the airline would have had to undergo huge expenses towards unloading our baggage, providing us with hotel accommodation, putting us back on their next evening flight and losing revenue for the two empty seats. The cost to the airline would have been significantly high. Repeated e-mails remained unanswered. The airline did not consider it necessary to show any flexibility. As a last resort, both I and my wife took membership in the airline's Frequent Flyer Program informing the customer relations executive. Promptly my account got credited with their offer of 50,000 miles. It was a unilateral decision and once again a demonstration of high handedness, I wrote back.

Finally, a Google search resulted in locating the name of the Vice President, Marketing & Customer Service of the airline. I searched on LinkedIn and locating him, sent a mail with the heading *'Business Class Customer Duped'*. I wrote down a short synopsis of the events that had followed. As compensation I demanded two return premier economy class tickets for me and my wife, equivalent to 70,000 miles in each membership account. The caption surely attracted attention and three days later, a conciliatory mail from Customer relations was received: our accounts had been credited with 2 x 70,000 miles.

Key Learning:

A Customer Relationship initiative mostly focuses on past purchase pattern resulting in potential customers getting eliminated. Differentiation amongst high-value and low-value customers can sometimes be offensive. These discriminations being common in the service industry cause satisfaction levels to drop considerably. In a service industry, every case should be handled cautiously, and every customer should be dealt with utmost care. Though the airline duly compensated us in the end, it failed to impress us.

Vignettes from My Diary

A London resident, an upper-class frequent flier of the same airline, had once boarded a flight to Delhi and just fastened his seat belt when he got a notification on his phone that the burglar alarm in his house had gone off. Not knowing what to do, he asked the cabin crew to let him get off the aircraft and bring out his luggage. They agreed to do it. He figured out later that such incidents cost the aircraft roughly Euro 150,000 - 200,000. The Airline, when demanded of it, had to do that for one passenger. However, the same airline chose not to extend the same courtesy to us and took advantage of my simplicity, tarnishing its name in the process.

9

Loyalty Regained

It was September 1995, the first-anniversary event of National Panasonic's entry in India. The dealers of the Delhi area were invited to a get-together at a 5-star hotel. By then the company had launched the locally manufactured economy model the 20-inch Top Dome Colour TV and Audio systems. It also introduced in the range a limited number of 70-inch large screen top-of-the-line GAO colour television – a direct one time import of a container load. The purpose was to enrich the range of Panasonic TVs and for a discerning customer to experience the technical competencies of Panasonic. The price difference between the two models was significantly high.

At the event, I walked up to Mr Ashok Madan, an eminent dealer at Karol Bagh, M/s India Radio and Electric whom I had known since my tenure with Philips India and BPL Sanyo Utilities. I wanted to chat about how he felt about the brand after a year of its launch. Disappointedly he replied, *'Mr Sengupta, with you being at Panasonic, I was expecting a much better response from the company, but I feel terribly let down and seriously debating of surrendering the Panasonic dealership'*. I was unprepared to hear this. In this competitive business environment, with several international brands vying for shelf space, it was difficult to make strong dealers accept the dealership of a newly launched brand. I had, all along, held great admiration for Mr Madan's awareness in the field of consumer electronics. We would often engage in long conversations, eager to exchange the latest developments in this field.

I asked Mr Madan what went wrong. He said that when the salesperson visited him a year back, he was persuaded to order one GAO CTV with other products in the Panasonic range knowing well there were very limited buyers those days for expensive sets and Karol Bagh may not be the right target market. When Mr Madan opened the packing box of the GAO set, the handset (remote control) was missing or misplaced by his shop assistant making the CTV completely unusable. He was unable to switch it on. As a result, the CTV was lying in the showroom as a piece of furniture. Mr Madan had brought the matter to the attention of the salesperson who, on his part, promised to investigate and supply the missing handset. Mr Madan also offered to pay, allowing the company the benefit of the doubt.

The salesperson, in turn, informed the Japanese product manager Mr Hosoi, who discussed it with the local marketing head. Over time, everything was forgotten and one year had passed. There was no follow-up action, neither the salesperson nor Mr Madan brought it to each other's attention. A concerted decision had been taken not to order the spares of this model from Japan since it was not planned for local assembly. Should a need arise, two or three GAO TV sets would be set aside to cannibalise their spare parts.

It was quite unusual for Japanese organisations to ignore a complaint. I told Mr Madan to allow me five working days' time to find a solution knowing well it would be tough. In this long period, no one knew the whereabouts of the CTVs that were set aside. The next morning, I met Mr Hosoi and narrated the incident adding that Panasonic would be losing an excellent dealer. Though we were not obligated to provide a free handset, it would be embarrassing at this stage to ask the dealer to pay. It was an arduous task for Mr Hosoi to locate a spare remote handset when possibly all the stocks of GAO CTVs had been sold out. While he was in continuous phone calls with all the warehouses, he was successful in locating one at Chandigarh and got it delivered to Delhi by a special messenger the next day.

Two days later the third morning, I took possession of the handset, telephoned Mr Madan and got it delivered the same afternoon. I also told him it would be complimentary. After the situation got closed, Mr Madan conveyed to me, *'Mr Sengupta, my confidence in Panasonic service is restored'.*

Key Learning:

'Promise only if you can deliver but deliver more than what you have promised' is a simple mantra.

Customers evaluate service delivery by its ability to be reliable and responsive. Reliability is the ability to perform the promised service dependably and accurately. Responsiveness is the willingness to help customers and provide prompt service. It is proven in this incident that customer's loyalty cannot be taken for granted.

Part Two

LEADERSHIP

A leader is not to be confused with a manager. The main difference between leaders and managers is that the leaders have people to follow them while managers have people to work for them. A successful business owner needs to be both a strong leader and manager to get their team on board to follow them towards their vision of success.

Managers and leaders are different but complimentary. Not everyone can be good at both leading and managing. Managers promote stability. They are patient listeners, do not take hasty decisions, and have lot of appetite for new ideas. Some can become excellent mangers but not strong leaders.

Being an effective leader entails having a vision of something larger than themselves as individuals developing a strategy, achieving the results through other people, and motivating them to execute the strategy. A leader's responsibility lies in creating a company culture and lastly, communicating all of the above to his team. He need not himself work hard or long or even efficiently (which means doing more things in lesser time with lesser inputs) – that is a manager's job.

The qualities of good leadership are:

1. The ability to get the right people in – people with a great value system. His own ability comes later.
2. The ability to get the wrong people out.
3. The ability to allow discussion within the team with no interruptions from the leader but also knowing when it is time to take the decision.

4. A decision once taken should be implemented remorselessly by the true leader, removing all barriers that come in the path including friends and relatives etc.
5. Getting the resources for the team.
6. Protecting the team from external badgering.

This is what worked under J Robert Oppenheimer when he led the Manhattan Project to make the Atom bomb. This is what Jim Collins writes in his book 'Good to Great'. This is what Jesus Christ – who now has the largest & wealthiest 'company' in the world that has lasted over 2000 years and is getting richer by the day – did. This is what the Buddha also did. Of course, this involves integrity; in fact, something more than integrity – probity.

Most great leaders do not decide – they allow the chosen team to decide. What the leader does is implement the decision taken by the chosen team with a very hard hand.

Look at the qualities of the leaders of companies that have beaten the stock market index consistently over a hundred years. These leaders often lack 'charisma'. The CEO of the largest company in the world in terms of revenue is Walmart & many have not even heard the name of Doug McMillon or of the CEO of the second largest company Sinopec.

No single book or workshop can teach how to be a good leader. Management knowledge can make better managers, but it is doubtful whether they create true leaders. Some of these leaders are a product of their environment and succeed in them. For the vast majority, it is a skill, self-learned by mindful attention to on-the-job experiences, job challenges, and all the external environments. Other than that, we know that some help from friends, bosses, mentors, and coaches can go a long way in making a leader go from good to great!

In the leadership stories that unfold in the following pages, the personalities who rose to the top positions were neither highly intelligent nor highly skilled individuals. They were very ordinary people, who may not have charisma, but they have just the right qualities to be leaders whom people respected and loved to work with.

(With inputs from Dr Tushar Roy)

10

Leadership in Uncertain Times

By Oscar Braganza

What is Leadership? What constitutes great Leadership? Who makes a great leader? Are leaders born or made? These and numerous other questions have been the subject of much management writing, and discourse over ages. The fact that we still study it, and we haven't yet found the perfect answer to these questions, leads me to believe that the Holy Grail is not yet in sight! Maybe the essence of great Leadership lies in this eternal Quest, *to move the boundary forward, move the bar higher, in a constant search for answers.*

In my work as a CEO Coach over the last 8 years and having worked with a number of my Coaches who come from very diverse industries, I have come across *2 strands of thought that are moving in different directions…*one is *the strand that is constantly evolving in the assessment of what constitutes great Leadership in the NOW…* the other is about those *aspects of leadership that are timeless*. Let me talk about the first evolving strand.

Leadership today necessitates the ability to be comfortable with Uncertainty. Covid induced challenges, have made us question the fundamentals… Our business models, the way we work, the way we survive etc. Being able to chart a course even when all the variables are not fully known…the ability to develop a compelling vision in the face of this uncertainty, and the passion, and humility to carry it through…maybe even change course if needed, by letting the ego get in the way, are some of the emerging imperatives of our times. This swiftness of being able to steer in variable time and periodicity without losing sight of the bigger picture has become a prerequisite of the world that we live in today.

With Uncertainty comes the need for Speed… The ability of a Leader to not always go for the perfect 100% academically correct course of action, which may take a huge amount of time to formulate, and is an ill afforded luxury in today's times, but to measure it against the cost of not acting, and then being overwhelmed by the force of circumstance. I am not arguing for trigger happy leaders, but for mindful leaders who pause briefly, and then act clearly and decisively…for whom working in an uncertain terrain has become an internalized operating principle.

With Speed and Uncertainty comes the Leader's need for Agility… The ability to see the key priorities, and the important moving parts in the holistic, and then form mission-critical crack teams for action. These teams then dissolve, once the task has been accomplished, to form new teams to tackle the next big challenge…the next set of leaders are right there in those teams, waiting to emerge onto a bigger stage. Empowerment of the individuals on these teams and of the teams themselves is fundamental to success. The ability to manage this agility is a new age requirement from Leaders.

And then there are *the timeless strands that constitute great leadership…* Honesty, Humility, Gratitude, Executive Presence, Empathy and Vulnerability make for the bedrock of great leaders. *To this, I would add one new age requirement… the ability to consciously work on oneself from within.*

How good is the Leader in *managing self*…his/her time, priorities, stress, moods, health, and energy levels? Is he/she creating enough quality me-time to 'sharpen the saw'? Do they have a personal routine or method to work on themselves… How strong is their Self-awareness of leadership style, and the impact that it is having on the team… With organizational structures in flux, how comfortable is the leader influencing and leading without authority, without being dependant on a title and the trappings of power?... When leading a highly competent team of sharp minds, conflict can become inevitable over the path forward. Managing conflict…being inclusive, is even more so in demand today than ever before.

The Leaders of today will always feel that they continue to be a work in progress, constantly evolving to a higher and higher plane of effectiveness. Those who feel, believe, and behave otherwise are doomed to be steering their companies over the cliff without even knowing it.

11

Trust Your Team, Be the Leader

It was a cold winter's Monday morning in the early 1970s, a time for the regular weekly meeting of the regional Product Sales Managers of Philips India with the Regional Manager at the Northern Regional Office, New Delhi. One such meeting was in progress.

Attendance to such meetings was compulsory, and in the event of any of the Product Sales Managers being absent, the second in charge took his place. The agenda would generally be a review of the progress in business and occasional announcement by the Regional Manager of any developments or changes in policy decisions. It was quite early in my career, and the subtle nuances of a true leader impressed me so much that I remember the details of that day's meeting vividly till today after so many years.

The meeting got suddenly interrupted when Regional Manager's secretary – an attractive middle-aged lady entered the room to inform him that the Philips dealer from Faizabad, M/s Nigam & Co wanted to speak with him urgently. The Regional Manager glanced at her and after pausing for a moment, considering that the meeting was already interrupted, asked her to put Mr Nigam on. With the phone receiver stuck to his ears, he heard Mr Nigam speak – venting out his anger perhaps because we could hear an agitated voice in that otherwise quiet conference room. Puzzled, we could not comprehend what the conversation was all about and looked at each other's faces. After a while, the Regional Manager abruptly ended the conversation with, 'Mr Nigam, the gratification to get a Philips Audio dealership ranged from Rs.25,000 to Rs.40,000.' He also added that he was shocked to hear that the Product Sales Managers of Audio, Mr Yogesh Mathur demanded only Rs.5,000 and that Mr Nigam could have heard him wrong.

It was nothing short of a bomb blast! The Regional Head smiled at all of us as he put the receiver down and continued with the meeting. It took us a while to bring back our mind to the point of the current discussion. We all overheard a part of a strange conversation. What had happened to warrant such a response?

The story was revealed only later by Yogesh Mathur. Faizabad in UP – now famous for the Ayodhya Temple – was an important market for Philips India, but our market share did not match with other districts in UP. The town was represented by only one dealer M/s Nigam & Co who had other interests too. He was a wine merchant and his focus on promoting the Philips brand left much to be desired. As a result, Philips was losing its market share. Repeatedly instructing and cautioning Mr Nigam did not help, and ultimately the Sales Executive who reported to Yogesh was advised to be on the lookout for a second option as an outlet. A couple of dealers had been shortlisted and a formal visit of Yogesh was required before finalisation. This call from Mr Nigam was made at this juncture. The approval for Dealership appointments was always routed through the Regional Manager before the actual appointment by the All-India Sales Manager at the Head Office in Bombay (now Mumbai). In almost all cases, the Regional Manager followed the mandate of the Product Sales Managers for dealership appointments.

Obviously, our dealer friend Mr Nigam felt insecure in such a scenario and out of revenge made this call, maligning Yogesh Mathur to his immediate senior. However, being a good leader that most of the Philips India senior managers were those days, the Regional Manager took charge of the situation and turned the conversation around to protect the image of his team.

I realised what it takes to be a good leader. Here are the pointers:

a) He took the call since it was referred to by his trusted and experienced secretary as an 'urgent' one while an important meeting was in progress – a demonstration of his priority to customers (In this case, a dealer) over any other matter.

b) In most circumstances, the customer would have been politely told that appropriate action will be taken after verifying the allegations, but here, the Regional Manager chose to articulate to Mr Nigam upfront in the presence of all other managers loudly and clearly that the person whom he was trying to implicate was in a way a stupid person to have demanded only Rs.5,000/-. The Regional Manager sent across a message to his team that he had complete trust in them.

Yogesh, at that time, had come from touring Lucknow where he had been responsible for Eastern UP sales – a very potent market. His performance was remarkable, and Philips' image was at its peak because of the efforts he had put in. Such was his reputation amongst the dealers that whenever he fell short of targets, he would simply call up a dealer on the phone and ask him to take additional orders, which the dealer would seldom refuse. They worked on mutual trust, and it was built over a period. Clearly, his efforts to create such goodwill was acknowledged by the senior management. He was brought to Delhi, the Northern Regional headquarters, subsequently.

A day before Diwali that year, Yogesh Mathur carried a bottle of premium Scotch – a rarity in the seventies – and visited the Regional Manager's residence to extend greetings. While reciprocating and accepting the bottle, the Regional Manager did not mince his words and asked, 'Why is this? Is it that you want a promotion?' Such was the bonhomie that was shared amongst the employees with the seniors those days. Everybody belonged to a team.

Later, following his retirement from Philips India after working for almost 35 years, the Regional Manager took up Philips Audio and Light dealership in Salem, Tamil Nadu where his ancestral home was. By then I had been posted to Chennai as the Regional Sales Manager for Audio products, Southern Region, and Tamil Nadu came under our Region's sales jurisdiction.

At one of my visits to Salem with the Sales Executive of that area, I visited his outlet. Such visits were a part of my regular job responsibilities. Upon seeing me, he came around his chair to greet me clasping both my hands, demonstrating respect to my position in Philips. He had been a very senior colleague of mine, but in this scenario, the roles had been reversed when he expressed, 'You are the principals, and I am your dealer'. I faced further embarrassment when trying to get him to sign an indent that I wished for as he demonstrated a tremendous amount of resistance, like any dealer. True to his new role and a professional to the core, he never allowed personal relationships to come in between. Later in the evening, he invited us over to his house for a drink.

Key Learning:

Trust does not occur overnight. The first two to three years of one's corporate career is critical. Performance, approach and attitude towards work, interpersonal skills and integrity are all keenly watched. A person becomes worthy of building trust when his/her track record has been consistent. Trust results in a collaborative environment getting the employee more committed to the jobs and this stimulates the group to high performance standards. The employee will be committed to bind himself to company decisions further. If you do not trust people, you make them feel insignificant and unworthy. How do you receive a commitment from him?

Human beings are primarily good by nature and possess the zeal to excel subconsciously and consciously when mentored.

(With inputs from Yogesh Mathur)

12

Nurture A Relationship
Part I: Beauty Lies in The Eyes of The Beholder

This mega event in the early days of my career is still etched in my mind – it was the Silver Jubilee meeting cum celebration of the Northern Regional Philips Radio Dealers Association (PRDA). The venue was Hotel Ashoka, Bangalore, and the year was perhaps 1975. The event was held for 3 days were attended by the Philips Radio (Consumer Electronics) dealers of Delhi, Haryana, Punjab, Rajasthan, and U.P. Managers, Sales Executives of the Region, the All-India Sales Manager, and the marketing team from the head office in Bombay (now Mumbai) along with the Marketing Director of the company also attended it. Most of the dealers were accompanied by their spouses.

During the day, arrangements were made for them to go out sightseeing and shopping whilst their husbands attended the meetings. There were some entertainment programmes in the evenings, followed by dinner. There would be much bonhomie as wine and champagne flowed.

On the last day of the meeting, the organising members of the dealers' association announced an unscheduled event

– a beauty pageant whose participants were to be the spouses of the dealers. At first, the ladies were reluctant and hesitant. Some of them vehemently objected to the idea. Most of them were shy, coming from small towns, and were never exposed to such an event in the seventies. However, the programme was scheduled and proceeded as planned. A ramp was created with the help of the hotel staff. Some of the ladies did not even know what walking in the ramp meant and needed to be convinced and assured again and again. Finally, about 35 of them mustered the courage to participate and came forward. The secretary of the PRDA members announced the names of the contestants and they were requested to line up. Immediately followed another announcement – the Marketing Director was going to judge the runner up and the winner. It was a shocker! The Marketing Director begged himself to be excused. It was quite clear from his expressions that he was completely unprepared and unaware of that evening's procedures.

Yet, as the leader of his team, he rose to the occasion and how! In the backdrop of soft music and under bright light, the ladies, draped in their choicest Bangalore silk sarees, probably purchased earlier in the afternoon, paraded in front of the large cheering audience. A show like this had never been witnessed before. Thundering clapping continued till the last of the participants presented themselves on the ramp.

When it was time for the Marketing Director to announce the names of the winners, he paused a bit. We, his junior colleagues waited with bated breath. How would he decide the winners? What criteria were set, and what was expected of these coy, homebound ladies most of whom were homemakers and did not have much exposure to the outside world? I was wondering what the outcome of his selection would be.

Probably everything was in his mind. He looked calm and started speaking in his own inimitable style, most humbly and modestly, 'Ladies and Gentlemen, in my long career with Philips India I have never found myself in a situation which has been as difficult as this; at the workplace or otherwise.' He continued, 'I believe like the poet; *Beauty*

lies in the eyes of the beholder. To every man, his wife is the most beautiful woman. Therefore, all the ladies who courageously participated in tonight's competition are worthy of a prize. I am awarding a Philips Radio to each one of the participants who together are the winners in this contest!'

The economy model Radio was a best seller those days and was extremely popular with the Indian consumers. It was a remarkable decision that came so spontaneously and left everyone stunned in delight. This is what made Philips a great place to work and for the dealers to be associated with. This kind of gesture of the top management made the dealers and the employees all remain a part of a big family.

Everyone was super friendly, every participant felt super happy and all of us still had the remainder of the evening left at the hotel to enjoy. As we all took the last sip of our drink, we and the dealer fraternity made a mental note: Philips' leadership was what made it a brand to cherish.

Nurture A Relationship
Part II: The Gruesome Train Accident

Another time, a different incident, at a different place, and the protagonist is another North Indian audio-radio dealer of Philips India.

A couple of years after Hotel Ashoka, Bangalore dealer meet, Northern India Patrika of 10th October 1977 published from Allahabad carried the headline: *'The Howrah-New Delhi express had rammed into a goods train at Naini station near Allahabad a little after midnight on October 9 killing 53 persons and seriously injuring another 86.'*

Unluckily, I was a passenger on the same train, though I, along with my mother and aunt and some of my fellow travellers, escaped unscathed. We were travelling on the ill-fated train in one of its air-conditioned coaches while returning from Kolkata and a newly appointed full-time household help was booked in the 3-Tier Sleeper non-AC coach of the same train. She was young, twenty-something, and could not speak a word of Hindi. I seated her in the coach and went and met her at every station that the train would stop. The Sleeper coach was next to the engine and ours was midway between the engine and the guard.

It was meant to be a long overnight journey and I met her at the last station before my mother, my aunt and I fell asleep. The outside was pitch dark when suddenly around the middle of the night, we were woken up from our

slumber with a big thudding sound with the train coming to a screeching halt with some of the overhead luggage falling over the shoulders of passengers and lights switching off. It must have been speeding at 70 kph or more. The position of our coach got tilted by 30 degrees to the right. Fortunately, no one was hurt in the compartment. Upon enquiry, we came to know that the train had halted close to Naini Junction near Allahabad. The dim lights of the platform could be seen at one far end. A large number of people had gathered outside, and different versions were being narrated – what was confirmed was that the train had met with an accident. They talked about heavy casualties and many were seen embracing each other and weeping out of shock. I was genuinely concerned about the young girl. Since her compartment was the first one following the engine, I walked towards it. All that I could see was the engine, and a first-class coach completely in a mangled and overturned position. There was a remote possibility of any survivor in those coaches. I was nervous. Amid all this, severely injured passengers were groaning with pain, they were shouting for help while some opportunist miscreants who had come by from nearby villages were robbing the passengers of their jewellery and valuables. It was a gory sight. I had never seen death from such close counters.

Help arrived from the railway soon. By about 3 AM passengers who had died were extracted with the help of welding machines and were arranged on the platform. Our maid could not be traced. I searched the mangled compartment, the railway track and wherever my intuition guided me to look for her, but she was not anywhere to be found. Wailing ambulances went past and an announcement was made that all the passengers would be taken in a rescue train to Allahabad station. Like zombies, we carried our belongings and boarded the train. Big suitcases and all our packed material were in the brake van which we were told would reach the station separately.

We reached Allahabad station around 6 AM and waited in the waiting room. After making my mother and aunt comfortable there, I hired a rickshaw to proceed to the only known face I could rely on at that time – our Philips dealer M/s Bhargava Engineering House at Civil Lines. I completely forgot the fact that my wife's uncle lived there in Allahabad – In any case, I didn't know his house or his address (those were the pre-mobile phone era), as I was married only a few years before that incident. On the other hand, I had often interacted with our Philips dealership. Mr Bhargava had a large single storey complex that housed a showroom, a conference room, a training room, and his residential quarters. M/s Bhargava Engineering were also Exide distributors of Eastern UP. That morning, I rushed into their house narrating the entire story starting from the untraceable young girl. He served tea and that steaming hot cup calmed my frayed nerves to a great respite.

Mr Bhargava's two sons who managed the business between themselves took out their cars and we searched all the hospitals of Allahabad where the injured could possibly be admitted. I could not spot her anywhere. I was giving up on hope. At that moment Mr Bhargava suggested why not we visit all the small hospitals too. As we visited them one after another, going from bed to bed, I spotted her finally in one of them, lying with an injured leg lifted at an angle in traction. She was fully conscious. She smiled and greeted me. I sighed, much relieved.

According to the attending doctor, she had multiple fractures in her leg and had to remain in the hospital for at least 3 weeks. As we drove back, my mind was still on the young girl and how to look after her in that situation. The dealer, as if reading my mind, said, 'We will take care of her at the hospital, relax and return to Delhi.' Our baggage had arrived by then and was kept in the luggage room. With my mother and aunt, we refreshed ourselves and the ladies of the house cooked a sumptuous brunch. A special train departing at 4 pm took us back to Delhi. The

Bhargavas were a very hospitable family that made us extremely comfortable in that emergency. I felt deeply touched as they dropped us at the railway station.

The young girl remained in Allahabad hospital under the scrutiny and care of the Bhargava's for three weeks. Later, her father came to escort her back to Kolkata. She was given some monetary compensation by the railways. This sums up the brotherhood of a Philips dealer – that could be seen through across India. There was an engaging bond. It had become the envy of our competitor.

Key Learning:

Philips organization's values and beliefs established by its leaders trickled down to its business partners levels. At every level of management, there was mutual trust and respect cementing the relationship, working in unison, each helping the other in times of need. When hard decisions had to be taken managers never shied away from their responsibility. Communication channels were always open. This is what made the company the top brand in those days and I was fortunate to have been a part of the team. The rock-solid relationship that we maintained with our dealership network was the competitor's envy.

The story is not a solitary episode. My relationships with the dealers endured till I left the organisation in 1990.

13

Inspire and Win

It was a case of the end justifying the act. Late in the evening on a Friday, the party in my house had just wound up, an office peon who obviously had consumed one drink too many was gathering the used glasses and plates in the kitchen. I felt sorry and bade him goodbye, asking another junior colleague to drop him home. The evening get-together was to celebrate the success of spare parts sales in our Northern Region Philips Service Centre that month.

When I took over as the Regional Service Manager in the Northern Region of Philips India in the mid-seventies, one of the key yardsticks of measurement of my performance was the bottom line. While revenue from Philips repairs was an insignificant component, spare parts sales were large. Higher spares sale reflected the use of more genuine spare parts over spurious parts used in repairs, a key to maintain our brand value. A comparison statement amongst the four regional offices Kolkata (East), Delhi (North), Mumbai (West) and Chennai (South) in India was circulated by the Head Office every month. Pressure from the head office mounted on the lagger. During my tenure, the Northern Region showed impressive results topping the chart for two consecutive years. In the two years preceding it was lower down. I then studied the situation and found that the old employees of the company were not motivated enough to book the spares orders as they felt it was not a part of their job. While out of office, their responsibility was only to provide support service to dealers and make a note of their spares requirement basis what the dealers said and upon return hand over the order to the supervisor of the spare parts. There was no effort to promote the sale of spares. After this finding I decided to let them be, instead tried to find out who was more forthcoming in this issue. Such staff members working inside the stores, namely the spare parts supervisor and the administrator, showed keen interest in travel and book orders. They had a good hold over the dealers who often visited the service centre to buy their spare parts.

But it was a more difficult proposition to sell this idea to the senior management. It was a deviation that could be questioned by the auditors later – a risk that I was ready to undertake, with the trust of my fellow colleagues of the Service Centre. For those who were travelling for the first time, it was a welcome break from their daily monotonous work and offered them a sense of job enrichment that was highly fulfilling. It rejuvenated them. When results started emerging, everyone appreciated our efforts. That is when I decided to celebrate with my junior colleagues. Once every four months, I would invite them over for dinner and drinks at my house. Lower cadre staff including peons, the sweeper, and the security staff – everybody was invited. It was a perfect way to bring cheers and a sense of belonging to their mundane routine. They were motivated and became part of a team complementing each other.

There were no provisions for staff entertainment in our budget, but a small amount was earmarked for dealer entertainment. When I asked for advice and approached the Regional Manager for funds for these get-togethers, the senior leader, winking at me said, 'Invite a couple of dealers too, that would set the record straight'. As my career grew in Philips, we learnt from seniors and imbibed leadership qualities and team management on the job.

Key Learning

To develop your career graph, you need to inspire and motivate your team and take responsibility for your team's actions. In an organisation, an individual without delegation cannot take responsibility, at the same time an individual with delegation cannot help but take responsibility.

This story is an example of infusing in the team a thrilling sense of being together in our ride, bringing excitement to the job and igniting their personal enthusiasm and commitment. The workplace, for all of us, was both a fun as well as a battleground setting. My team was with me in it together not only for the sake of the job but for the fun of it too.

14

His Fault, Their Fault, Not Mine

I was one of the first few to join Panasonic India in 1994 when the Japanese multinational Matsushita Electricals (National brand) set up their operations under the name Panasonic India Ltd. I was the head of the after-sales-service operations. Panasonic made a foray into Consumer Electronics with their CTVs and Audio systems, collaborating with an Indian partner at that time. We were a team of 8, working at the head office at Greater Kailash II, New Delhi. And another 5 at the Delhi branch which also functioned from the same premise. We launched the 21' flat screen Top Dome model, extremely popular back then in South East Asia. It cost Rs.18,000 at that time.

The Service Centre also undertook repairs of all imported National products through the network of National Authorised Service Centres across India. This facility existed before the setting up of the local Panasonic office and was supervised from Japan. National Panasonic was a popular brand amongst the returning NRIs those days.

Colour televisions bought from the United Kingdom did not adhere to the standard broadcast system here in India. Europe and India, follow PAL B (Phase Alternating System) whereas the UK follows PAL I. A component referred to as the 'tuner' in the CTV set made the main difference.

Sometimes in May 1995, a UK returned doctor attached to Batra Hospital in New Delhi visited our workshop with a Panasonic television set purchased at Cambridge in the UK prior to his shifting location here. He complained that the CTV was not functioning at his residence in South Delhi. We had anticipated this and verified after reading the instruction manual, that it was a PAL I CTV. The doctor, however, was not aware of this. He said that before leaving the UK he had confirmed with the Panasonic office in London and was told that the model would work in India. We were in a predicament about whether to believe him or not. Maybe the doctor was calling a bluff or the UK office personnel were ignorant of the broadcast system in India and casual in answering the doctor. Whatever be it, we respected the customers' anguish. Adachi San (San means 'Mr' or 'Ms' in Japanese), the Japanese head responsible for after-sales service of Indian and imported products, after a thoughtful discussion, allowed the customer the benefit of the doubt. One senior engineer was put on the job to replace the 'tuner' component with a local one used in the local Top Dome CTV. This would need some modifications/ alterations in the electronic circuit board and an improvised tuning knob was attached externally to the CTV spoiling its looks. The doctor gave us the 'go ahead' for this change, and the engineer got on to the job and struggled to fix the tuner at an appropriate place. A good amount of 'juggad' was involved that cost money and other resources. The doctor agreed to all proposals as otherwise, it was going to be an 'idiot box' in the true sense for him.

A circular knob for changing channels was mounted on the side of the cabinet. The doctor arrived to collect the TV set and a successful demonstration was given. The doctor was advised how the picture and sound could be put to near perfection by adjusting the knob. The customer looked pleased while taking delivery of the CTV and was overwhelmed with joy when we told him it was for free. The total amount of money spent by the company at that time was around Rs.5000/-. We followed the Konusuke Matsushita dictum 'Happy customer, happy employees.' I re-checked the performance of the CTV set every two days for a few days.

Ten days later, I noticed the same doctor entering the Service Centre with the CTV held by an assistant. He dumped it on the reception desk and said that he was 'fed up' as the CTV required constant fiddling and adjusting the knob. I asked, 'What do you want us to do next?'

He replied, 'I don't know, your UK office misguided me, and as far as I am concerned whether it's Panasonic UK or India, it's the same. You have to find a solution.' Arguments and counter-arguments continued for a length of time – Whose fault, was it? The doctor did not remember who he spoke with at the London office. Maybe he was trying to take advantage of the situation. Half an hour into this conversation, Shinozuka San, the Managing Director, who was keenly observing us from a distance, signalled that I meet him. He wanted to understand the situation and I narrated it in detail. At the end of it, he said with his soft voice 'Sengupta San, replace the CTV with our locally manufactured Top Dome for free.' I was taken aback. I said 'Shinozuka San, you don't know Indian customers, the doctor is possibly taking advantage of us.' Embracing my shoulder he said, 'Sengupta San, how many such cases would you get in a year- one or two, right? Panasonic can bear such costs to make customers happy. Allow the doctor a benefit of the doubt.'

Instructions were issued to replace the colour television with the local Top Dome CTV. It took about half an hour for the paperwork to be completed. The doctor thanked us abundantly and left our premises looking grateful, with a big smile on his face.

What followed thereafter was spectacular. The word-of-mouth amongst the doctor fraternity at Batra Hospital spread like wildfire. In the following two months we received a request for quite a few of Panasonic Top Dome CTVs from other doctors enhancing the Panasonic brand image. Thanks, Shinozuka San for your leadership.

Key Learning:

In one of the HBR's must-read on 'Strategy', a few lines are worth quoting – 'The Japanese have a deeply ingrained service tradition that predisposes them to go at great lengths to satisfy any need a customer express.' I noticed they do not indulge in the blame game but find out the problem and fix it. Everybody makes mistake, and what is different is that you accept the mistake, find ways to correct it and avoid recurred ones. That is what the Japanese have in their working styles. While talking about why something is wrong, they are calm and focus on solving the problems. The seniors make employees feel a part of the team who in turn work far harder to get the team out of the predicament.

15

Work First, Family Second

I was travelling with the Personnel Manager to recruit staff for our Kolkata office during my stint with National Panasonic between 1994 –96. We were working from the hotel room where we were lodged as office premises had not been finalized then. The shortlisted candidates were being interviewed one by one when suddenly the Personnel Manager received a call from his wife that their baby daughter had fallen sick and required hospitalization suddenly. He called up the Panasonic office in Delhi and requested one of his junior colleagues to go home and help his wife and provide for all the necessary arrangements. Obviously, his colleague obeyed his boss's instruction. The junior rushed out of the office after informing the Japanese head. Fortunately, the baby's illness did not turn out to be a serious one and by the end of the day, the mother-daughter duo was home safely. Though we continued with the interview, I could see that the Personnel Manager was disturbed. A day later, both of us returned to Delhi after completing our assignment.

Upon reaching office the next day, the Personnel Manager was questioned by the Japanese head. He was admonished for using an office resource for attending to personal work during office hours. The Personnel Manager tried to explain the circumstances, but the Japanese boss refused to be convinced. He said clearly that it was not how Japanese management worked.

The Personnel Manager realised that unlike in our country, work comes first in Japan and family second.

Just a couple of years later, I faced a similar situation in my life. By then I had switched jobs and had joined Usha International in Delhi. Ten days into my induction program at Usha International, I was to visit the Divisional offices as a part of that program. My mother who was staying near Kolkata then suddenly fell ill and I needed to go and visit her urgently. I did not have the courage to inform my Senior Executive Director and ask for leave. Another colleague with whom I was sharing a large office cabin looked at me and sensed that something was bothering me. He asked if everything was alright and I told him that my mother was not well and that I did not have sufficient cash left with me at that time and debating whether I could go during my induction program – I was so new to the organisation.

A little later, the Senior Executive Director came to know about my dilemma. He suddenly called me to his office. He inquired about my mother's health and asked if I needed some money. Sensing my hesitation, he said they were making some changes in my induction schedule to the Divisional offices, and I could prioritize my visit to Kolkata over the other offices. Not only this, he also went ahead and instructed the finance department to offer sufficient travel advance to me to take care of my expenses during the trip.

These two stories exemplify the work cultures of the two South Asian countries – Japan and India. Though in the first case the Personnel Manager of Panasonic India should have first informed the Japanese head, instead of asking for help from a colleague directly, the Japanese head's reaction should have been more humane. After all, the workplace occupies a major part of an employee's waking hours. It is, therefore, desirable that at time of need, the workplace is the first point of contact for employees.

At the same time, it is not fair to think that the Japanese are without emotion. On the contrary, they are an extremely helpful race. But as they are very disciplined too, they go out of the way to help others outside their working hours. I had experienced it during my Japan visit. There are plenty of instances when the Japanese people, on their way home from work in the late evening, tired and possibly hungry, would take a detour to help me find my way to the hotel where I was staying. Once a Japanese tourist guide (*Top left picture in story 6: Customer Experience: The Japanese Way*) personally escorted my wife and me in a bullet train after his duty hours were over, literally going out of his way, to ensure that we reached our destination safe and sound. But when it concerned work, the same Japanese would become a strict disciplinarian.

16

When I Met Mr. Ratan Tata

By Prakash Waknis

1990, I became responsible for Philips Car Stereo Business because of the resignation of my predecessor. It was a single product business with a sales value of Rs. 30 Million and 15 per cent gross profit. We were told that we would get no resources to develop new products and need to source products from the market. After about 6 months of working in this department, my colleague Vinay and I identified a product, and it was released only to be ridiculed. This was in July 1991. Around August 1991, we received a call from TELCO (Now Tata Motors). They wanted to fit this product in their LCVs, TATA 407 and 608. We fitted it in a vehicle and gave a demonstration. We also prepared a photo album detailing step by step process of fitting. This worked. We started supplying the product in October 1991. The purchase order was for 40,000 pieces to be supplied over the next 12 months. It was valued at about Rs 110 million which translated to a gross profit of Rs 30 million.

Suddenly everyone in the company started taking notice of this. Resources were assigned from the factory. Before this, no one in the factory knew about the process of managing the OEM (Original Equipment Manufacturer) business. The business continued with minor hitches till March 1993.

First interaction with Mr Ratan Tata.

I received a call while I was on leave in Mumbai – 'Mr Waknis, the order is cancelled. Stop supplies immediately.' I tried to find reasons. But the person at the other end said 'Instructions'. I returned to Pune where my office was and met my colleague to share the bad news. We also informed the factory procurement group. We wrote letters to the CEO of Telco's Pune unit. No response. Sent them a reminder – still no response. Two weeks had passed like this. I was to be transferred back to Mumbai, but I did not want to leave an unfinished job. I sent the same letter to Mr Tata in their Mumbai office. There was no response.

Let us backtrack a little. In 1991, Mr, Ratan Tata was honoured as CEO of the decade. I had sent him a congratulatory letter. He, graciously, as he is famed to be, responded by a letter on the expensive, personalised letterhead. Now, I had his autograph. Having (almost) lost all hope, I sent a fax to Mr Tata describing the unfairness of the decision. By now we were almost in the middle of June 1993, three months after the cancellation of the order and still there was no response. Desperate that I was, I sent a reminder by fax to Mr Tata. As far as I can remember now, it was a Thursday. The following Saturday, I got a call from TELCO. The conversation roughly followed like this:

TELCO – 'Mr Waknis? xxx here.'

Me – 'Yes Mr xxx.' This was the same person who was very curt to me in March 1993.

TELCO – 'How are you Sir?' (I noticed the 'Sir' suffix). He continued after my casual 'Fine', 'You can resume supplies as per the schedule given for the next three months. We have decided this to help you plan your procurement.' I again noticed the words 'help you plan'.

Me – 'Please send a fax to that effect with a clear delivery schedule.'

TELCO – 'Yes Sir. By the way, Mr Waknis, may I ask a question?' And after my go ahead, 'Do you personally know Mr Ratan Tata? We got a very terse instruction from him today.'

I just said, 'Maybe,' and disconnected.

On the same day, there was a party to bid farewell to our expat boss known for his sceptic attitude. When everyone was appreciating my efforts my outgoing boss in his characteristic cryptic tone asked me, 'So you are happy. What would you have done if Mr Tata had not responded?' I answered back – 'I don't respond to hypothetical questions.' He walked away red faced.

Face to face interaction with Mr Tata

In 1992, we had launched a digital feature-packed car stereo with an anti-theft feature. At the same time, Telco had launched Tata Sierra and Estate cars – also feature-packed. So now we proposed the new product. The engineering team at Telco was quite happy and recommended it. But the price was a hurdle at that time. Let me go into a bit of detail. Those days, the excise on cars was 40 per cent while excise on our product was at 20 per cent. But once it is integrated into the car, the excise on the car stereo would go up and affect the price (of the car) adversely. On this ground, our proposal was turned down. Now we wrote to Mr J E Talaulikar, the MD of TELCO and then met him. It was my first interaction with a great person. When we entered his office, he came around his chair and shook hands. Gave us a patient hearing and examined the product. And said, 'Looks impressive. But, as Vinay, my colleague and I braced for another 'NO', he continued, 'I am not a technical person. I suggest you meet our chairman. 'I will make arrangements for that.' He advised his assistance to fix up a time and gave us one car to fit the stereo. Two days later, the car arrived, and the stereo was fixed. The appointment with Mr Tata was confirmed at 9.30 AM on the coming Saturday.

We reached Mr Tata's residence in Colaba. After introductions, Mr Tata surprised me by asking me, 'Are you the Mr Waknis who sent me a reminder by fax? Not many do it and get away by doing this act.' He smiled. Then he listened to our description of the car stereo carefully and nodded in appreciation. 'Nice. Can you come with me Mr Waknis? Let me show my Buick'. We then sat in the car and he started the stereo in his Buick. He was playing our demo cassette. It sounded great. It had 16 speakers, 4 per channel, 4 speakers per channel. Mr Tata looked at us. I said 'Great sound sir. If you fit our system here, it would sound equally good.' I did not know then, but I had walked into a trap. Mr Tata switched off the system and said, 'Precisely'. We got out of the car and started walking back to the parked Sierra where two senior managers from Telco were gaping at us. When we reached the car Mr Tata continued, 'Precisely, Mr Waknis. This car (he pointed toward Sierra) is not worth your excellent product. Also, it does not fit into our pricing strategy.' What a way to say no! Our faces (Vinay's and mine) must have registered disappointment. Mr Tata threw back his head and laughed. 'Hey, don't feel bad. I am instructing our salespeople to strongly suggest that your product should be our first choice for retrofitting. It was nice meeting two young and energetic guys. Give my regards to Mr xxx (Philips MD).'

Surprisingly, we started getting orders from Telco dealers. Our purpose was partially served.

Key Learning:

This is a story of how relentless efforts always have a positive outcome. If one does not get what one wanted in the first place, the satisfaction of trying cannot be measured in simple terms. Some takeaways:

1. *Never take no for an answer. Do not give up till all means have been exhausted.*

2. *Never have any inhibitions while interacting with Chairmen/MDs. They are also humans.*

3. *Honesty in the efforts always gets a reward. It may not meet your expectations. But there is a great satisfaction of having 'tried like hell' even in case of failure.*

17

Good Boys Also Win

By Gautam Sen

Lee Iacocca, the legendary CEO of Chrysler Corporation describes his former boss Henry Ford II at Ford Motor Company as a 'first-rate bastard' in his autobiography. Examples of individuals with little human values who reach the top of the career ladder abound. This is true for all professions – corporate career, law, medicine and even sports. Many examples can be cited when a potential rival has been eliminated by an individual to further his own cause. The likes of Aurangzeb by and large rule all professions.

The objective of this story is not about the blood-thirsty and mean professionals. On the contrary, it is about personalities who have thrived in the professional jungle without compromising their integrity and moral values. These people have not harmed a soul and yet reached the pinnacle of their respective careers whom I have personally known over decades.

Dr Ajay Kohli – a chair professor of Marketing at the Georgia Institute of Technology, Deepak Goyal – a partner and MD with BCG at the New York office and Anand Kripalu – the present MD of Diageo plc India are such stars. I have observed key similarities in them and yet there exists remarkably diverse uniqueness in their professional conducts that differentiate them. The reader if they are in the process of building their careers can possibly take a cue from these individuals. Even today there are ethical ways of climbing the career ladders.

The Similarities.

All three individuals came from upper-middle-class backgrounds. The fathers were employed with Government enterprises – Indian Airlines, Professor at IIT Delhi and the Indian army, respectively. They attended good schools but not the elitist ones such as the Doon School or the Woodstock School. All of them went to IITs to study Engineering and later after working as Engineers for two to three years went on to attend the IIMs. Ajay and Anand attended IIM Calcutta while Deepak joined IIM Ahmedabad.

All three were very lively individuals participating in hosts of extracurricular activity starting from music to sports. They were kind-hearted and were always ready to help friends and were well-liked in any group they mixed. They were never bookworms but enjoyed life in every sense.

All three, while being confident of their own abilities, never dreamt of reaching the heights they have reached in their formative years. There was always the self-doubt which created the Kinetic energy in them to fulfil the potential they had. They really became self-actualized.

The Mantras They Live By

One is a professor, another a Consultant while the third has a corporate career. Let us look at the mantras they practice. For Ajay, the priority is 'thought leadership' in his research work. Deepak says his priorities are learning and unlearning and Anand says he/ is proud to utter in group meetings the phrase 'I don't know'. Probing deeper all three are saying the same. 'Thought leadership' comes by unlearning the past and opening new frontiers. This is the same as Deepak's quest for 'learning and unlearning' or Anand as the MD and CEO learning from a young manager's thought process. All three are continuously learning and unlearning to adapt to the newer world.

Anand works to create a legacy. The legacy is not only the size and the quality of the balance sheet. He says legacy is the management quality he will leave behind so that seamless transfer of the baton can happen. He is talking about subordinate development. So is Ajay when he says that his key priority is 'giving back to the community' through the development of his doctoral students. (His students are senior professors in B Schools across the globe). Deepak says that his priority is to 'spot winners and groom them'. Though articulated differently, all three put huge effort and focus to develop the next level of leadership and management talent.

Yes, for all three the continuous endeavour to learn/unlearn and subordinate development are passions. The aspiring CEOs may please take a note.

Key Learning:

These examples are of individuals who have attained great heights in their chosen profession. They are the epitome of a good soul and devoid of any manipulative behaviour. The noteworthy commonalities amongst them are: their individual background, being always helpful, humility and no show-off or flamboyance.

18

From Football Field to Corporate Board Room

By Gautam Sen

IIM Ahmedabad instituted a study on the Dabbawallas of the Bombay local trains. The president of the Dabbawalla association was invited to deliver a talk to IIM on the mastery of supply chain management. The art and science of supplying Dabbas is also a case study in Harvard Business Review (HBR). Companies sharpened their supply chain operations with learnings from the operation to improve productivity.

Similarly, could the methods of Alex Ferguson the legendary Professional Manager of Man U (Manchester United) in England be transplanted to create a corporate strategy? Let us investigate.

Is it possible? Can the building blocks of the management of a Football team hold good? What are the common threads? If we define Football or sport in general as an entertainment business, then perhaps it falls in line. HBR has also published articles on the management style and content of Alex Ferguson.

Some areas of convergence are:

The Supply Line of Talent

Professional Sportsmen have a limited lifespan of about a decade. The talent pipeline has to keep pace with the exits. Scouting and nurturing talent from an early age, therefore, becomes critical. Alex Ferguson persuaded the Man U board to make huge investments in this area of their youth program. None questioned the wisdom. Over twenty years Man U won 38 trophies under Ferguson. Similarly, corporates refurbish their talent needs by trying to develop a robust line of entry-level talent pool. The health of a company is dependent on the managerial bench strength and its leadership development program.

In India, the Fabled Management Training Program of Hindustan Unilever has produced possibly the maximum number of CEOs across businesses. In America GE till a decade back was the nursery for the best Business Leadership.

Dare to Rebuild

Alex Ferguson challenged the status quo when he took over Man U in 1986. He inherited a failing Football Club and turned that into the most valuable Football Club in History. (Forbes estimates the value at over 3 billion USD when he left). He overhauled the existing system and put focus on a mix of home-grown talent and few expensive purchases from other clubs unlike its city rival ManCity (Manchester City) who predominantly relied on the acquisition of ready-made footballers who were at their prime.

Great companies around the world have excelled by promoting leadership roles from within . Examples in

India include Hindustan Unilever or a GE in America (till it fell in bad times in the last decade). HUL and GE restructured their operations exiting traditional businesses. HUL in India sold the Dalda brand (it was known as the Dalda Company) and GE sold most of its appliance and lighting businesses.

Creating a Team of Winners

Ferguson over the years created a team that wanted to win. Under him, Man U won the English Premium League thirteen times. Also, the number of times the team came from behind to win the match in the last ten minutes of a game is a part of folklore. Each member of the team believed that they are ordained to win. A combination of extremely gifted players when put together did not win titles but a lesser gifted lot, won it when they played as a team complimenting each other.

The winning mentality exists among the leaderships of excellent companies. The will to win is exhibited in the corporate culture in the worst of adversity. There is no arrogance but supreme self-belief. This can be spotted in the junior-most manager to the CEO of the company. The will to win becomes an infection and it spreads to all.

No Hero Culture

Alex Ferguson threw out David Beckham at the height of his ability when he was the captain of England with a huge personal fan following. The action was taken because he started behaving bigger than the team and had a highly publicised and celebrated star lifestyle.

Look around the excellent companies and you will not find a group of Rock stars. There could be a couple of stars – internally but to the outside world, it is the face of the CEO. GE had only Jack Welch and in the Tata Group, it was only Ratan Tata. Incidentally, Ratan Tata purged the group satraps when he took over. Heavyweights like Rusy Mody (Tata Steel), Darbari Seth (Tata Chemicals) or A. Kerkar (India Hotels) were eased out.

Eye the Future Not the Moment

'He's never really looking at this moment, he's always looking into the future – knowing what needs strengthening and what needs refreshing – he's got that knack,' said the former Man U and England player Ryan

Giggs about Sir Alex. The introduction of a complete medical facility inside the Man U stadium or the introduction of yoga to increase physical and mental fitness were initiatives that Ferguson took much before anyone else in the sport.

Board rooms looking at a decade in advance rather than the quarterly result stand out. HDFC group's play in all aspects of the financial system starting from the HDFC Bank, Insurance and Asset Management company has made the company a powerhouse in the financial sector. Nurturing the businesses under unlisted entity and building the businesses for a decade before going public has provided huge upsides for shareholders.

Yes, the best practices from the English Premier League can be borrowed by Corporate Management. Just the way IPL in cricket is a case study on Brand Building.

So, per se, a football team and its coach can teach a trick or two to the men in the pinstriped suits in the ornate boardroom. Three best practices from a professional football club are: Spotting extraordinary talent, forming a team with incredibly talented individuals, and providing a psychological contract to the creative geniuses.

Get the Talent:

Creative businesses (movie studios and advertising agencies) do not have the luxury to rely on a supply chain of the talent pool from the Harvard/MIT, IIM/IITs as a McKinsey or Boston Consulting Group (BCG) does. I am not suggesting that BCG does not do creative work. However, the creativity of the management consultants come to play after they complete 15 years on the job whereas in an advertising agency the real stars possibly get burnt out after 15 years of work – just the way an ace footballer gets past his prime after fifteen years of professional football. Hence the talent for a Man U must be spotted when the individual is possibly 17 years of age, still in school and it must be found from a much wider net. George Best joined Man U when he was spotted playing football in Belfast, not well known for its football nursery. In much the same way, Piyush Pandey found his way in advertising from a tea testing room. There is no season for recruiting such talent as against the selection time of the management institutes at the end of February. The challenge is to be on the lookout for that heavy uncut diamond from all walks of life.

Forming a Team with Stars:

It is not easy to manage Real Madrid with Ronaldo, Beckham, and Zidane. Closer home, the NDTV system could not hold together Pranay Roy, Rajdeep Sardesai and Arnab Goswami. However, if someone could hold these incredibly talented individuals together and could use each one of them to complement each other's skills, there would be no possibility of the offshoot news channels. If only Pranay Roy acted as a coach rather than the best newsreader and had adapted the skills of Alex Ferguson, the stars would have stayed back. Make no mistakes – the stars did not leave for only money. The psychological contract was missing.

Create the Psychological Contract:

In international football, S. Gerrard was all set to leave Liverpool but he stayed back after the high he had after winning a tournament in Istanbul while T. Henry reversed his decision and stayed back in Arsenal after playing in the losing side in Paris. What made them reverse the decision – nothing else but a psychological contract. It was the way the coach spoke to them after/before the match. It was the way fans cheered them, perhaps it was the way the fellow players hugged them when they scored a goal. An astute coach fosters such feelings, ensures that the love and affection for the stars are exhibited openly and above all, they are made to feel wanted. Make no mistake – the stars are paranoid about a reduction in their fan following. The crux of the matter as to why Ogilvy has remained at the forefront in creative work in India is because Piyush Pandey ensures that the psychological contract gets renewed and reinforced every moment, every day – 365 days in a year at least with the creative team.

Remember the way Alex Fergusson handles Man U off the field and the way the stars respond to his teachings on the football pitch and the trophies they win decide the stock price of Man U. No wonder it is the wealthiest corporate football club in the world in terms of market capitalization. Chelsea, perhaps, has toppled the applecart but that is another story.

Part Three

SALES

Marketing is 'Doing the Right Things' and Sales is 'Getting the Things Right.' Marketing is generating a desire for our products, selling is converting the desire into a transaction and linking the two is a service that transforms those transactions into satisfied clients.

Selling is Vital to Our Business

No matter how good our product or service, it will not sell itself. We might sell a little simply because people have heard of us but sustained turnover and profits will only happen if we keep that vital link with customers by selling.

Selling our products and services is the most important activity of our business because without sales we make no profits. The two main selling situations ie legacy marketing have been: customers come to us, or we visit them. If customers come to us, they are already in a buying frame of mind and expect to be 'served', that is, they expect to have help in buying. The difference between legacy marketing and selling and online selling can be seen by a fundamental change of wording. Instead of determining what customers need it is determining what the customer needs – the individual customer – then satisfying those needs with specific products or services at the 'right' price, delivered directly to the customer.

Personal selling is the most powerful, but we must be reasonably sure that the person is a prospective buyer and not possibly waste our time trying to sell to someone who is not the decision-maker. Supposing we travel some distance to see a company we think could be a client and during our interview find that they have no need of our service. That could have been established that by an e-mail or telephone call. Selling products, and especially services, by e-mail/ telephone, is usually between known parties: the receiver knows or knows of the caller and the product or service being offered. The unsolicited sales calls that we receive from time to time get very annoying and does not portray a good image of the brand.

The Born Salesman

In one of the companies that I worked at, there was a laid-out well-established procedure of an office procedure, without which, no monetary sanctions could be given. It had to be approved by the heads of marketing, finance, accounting, IT, and finally the Chief Executive. The most arduous task was obtaining the sanction from the Finance Head who would nit-pick every detail with a magnifying glass and even made alterations to the script before he signed.

The marketing department had formulated an incentive scheme for its dealers for achieving an increased sales target. One of the Sales Office Heads wanted some specific relaxation in the scheme and approached us at the head office to say that it would enable more dealers to enjoy the benefits. We did not agree as the scheme was drafted after a lot of thought and with a certain objective in mind. Any deviation would only dilute the process and would be too risky if the quantities failed short of their target. This salesperson, six-foot-something tall, showed up at our office on one of the monthly visits and attempted to convince us face to face. Sensing that we would not give in to his request, while his turn arrived to meet the finance head, he walked into his office, sat there for some time, and came out of the Finance Head's cabin dangling a piece of paper announcing, 'I got it done.' He succeeded in convincing how his proposal would result in a winning situation for the company. The sales process for these born salesmen would be as ordinary as breathing is to you and me. They possess a 'fire under their belly.'

The natural-born must recognize their skills and put themselves in a position to use them. It just means we must be more conscious and more deliberate of the sales process and more mindful of what we do, being open to new ideas and approaches, and willing to at least try things outside our comfort zone.

What Every Salesperson Should Know…

Products and Customers

What customers regard as 'value' and what they buy is decisive – it determines the nature of a company's business, what it produces, and whether it will prosper. Customers are the foundation of a company; without them, it fails. This is the real purpose of marketing and selling: *to find customers*. Profit reflects the success of finding and satisfying them.

A company's products must be related to its target markets and attractive enough in appeal, performance, and price for customers to buy. Customers are sometimes unaware of their wants and these must be aroused. The ballpoint pen was not needed, it was not wanted, it was not a yearning in customers' minds; its flexibility and advantages over ink pens had to be demonstrated and a need created. What customers buy is what you should be selling.

Amongst different elements to a successful sale, one is attitude. The way you present yourself, your posture, your clothing, your tone, even the way you look at a customer gives off subtle signals. The second is the art of collaboration and relationship focusing both inside and outside the company. This approach produces superior, predictable, repeatable business results.

Putting the customer first requires caring for the customer, finding harmony in the sales relationship, having high moral ethics, being faithful to one's word and fair in the sale.

(With inputs from Dr Len Rogers)

19

Opportunity Doesn't Wait

Browsing through my bookshelf, my eyes converged on 'Think and Grow Rich' and that took me down memory lane. It was gifted to me by one of the Directors of Solidaire India in Madras (now Chennai) when a week before I was leaving their company. This book contains money-making secrets that can change one's life. I presume he wanted to imply that there never was a time when self-analysis and individual thinking were more important than at that juncture of my life. On the front page of the book was inscribed,

> *'To: S. Sengupta - At the crossroads in March 1988, this book will give you new insight.*
>
> *With Affection*
>
> *A.S Ramana Prasad, 11- March- 1988'*

Let me start with the background of this story. I had joined Solidaire TV in 1986 after working for 17 years with Philips India. It was a family-managed company with a sales turnover of approximately Rs.50 Cr at that time. Solidaire was the *'numero uno'* brand in Tamil Nadu followed closely by Dyonara those days. I was chosen as the General Manager responsible for sales and marketing. This was the first time the company appointed an outside professional to expand their business. My responsibilities were to explore new markets, new avenues of sales and ramp up turnovers.

On the first day of my assuming office, the younger of the two brothers, A S Ravi Prakash, responsible for Marketing and Sales led me to his plush cabin and handed over charge offering me, *'This seat is yours henceforth, and here you go...'* Within a month, I got well-established and travelled with Ravi Prakash to their dealers in South India where they had a good stronghold. Business increased and so did my confidence with the family members. The Technical Director of the company was Anoop Kumar, a close associate of the family who was responsible for design and production. He was a techie of that time. He had handpicked Pranab Basu from the Philips factory in Kolkata and made him in charge of production. Gradually, processes got streamlined and the turnovers increased to Rs.65 Cr in the following year as we expanded our network into other states. There was, however, a stark difference between how we sold in Philips and Solidaire. In Philips, we chased sales and dealers always paid up on time. At Solidaire our targets were 'day's collections', not sales. Sales followed collections. The company concentrated on institutional sales and it was generally Ravi Prakash's domain. This was an avenue that gave a quantum jump to the top line. Ravi Prakash had good connections. Each order would fetch 50 to 300 TV in one shot.

I was provided with a company accommodation at a Rishikesh Apartment complex near Panagal Park in Madras (it wasn't Chennai yet), a centrally located area.

Unlike most apartments in Chennai of the eighties, quite a few of the inhabitants were of North Indian origin. This made us feel comfortable. We became friends with Deepak and Teena Raj and their family. They ran a garment business. Our sons got along and played with the neighbour's children. One evening the cricketing legend Kapil Dev had come over to the Raj's' place and my sons were thrilled to have a look at him.

Politician and film actor M G Ramachandran (MGR) who served as the Chief Minister of Tamil Nadu and was most popular amongst the masses died on 24 December 1987 in Chennai before his 71st. birthday. People reacted to grief in a strange way then – it sparked off a frenzy of looting and rioting all over the state. Chennai city was no exception. It was shut with nothing functional. The city was in a curfew-like situation with offices, shops and establishments closed. The concept of working from home did not exist in those days. I was becoming restless and went across to Deepak's house for a chat and asked him whether he had some beer. He said no but suggested, 'Let us go to Hotel Chola'. He knew the General Manager well and was sure we could help ourselves with a bottle. The GM's name aroused curiosity in my mind as I had heard Hotel Chola was looking for CTV sets for their rooms. Many 5-star hotels were coming up in Chennai those days. I had also heard that Dyonara had already clinched the order through advance information and networking. Hotel Chola was near our house. With no available transportation, akin to the lockdown situation caused by COVID 19 pandemic, we could only walk down, but the consideration of walking a length of around 3 kilometres was very scary. Anything could happen to anybody. Arson

and looting had taken place in nearby areas. However, we developed courage, sought permission from our respective spouses, and walked hands clutched together amidst stone splattered streets on way to the Hotel. No one could be seen around us. It took us 20 odd minutes of a brisk walk to reach and at the reception, we asked for the GM (Khanna). Mr Khanna came and greeted us, Deepak introduced me to him, and we told him the purpose of our visit. He apologised and said, 'The bar is closed today'. Was the effort we took all in vain? Upon our insistent request, he offered to open one spare room for us where we would be served beer privately. That is exactly what we needed at that time. The waiter brought a few bottles and snacks to munch.

Mr Khanna and I became quite pally as both of us hailed from New Delhi. After we finished a bottle each, I enquired of Mr Khanna, 'Was there a requirement of 100 colour television sets @ Rs.9000/- from your hotel to be equipped in each of your rooms and the order had been issued to Dyanora?' He did not deny, but there was a caveat and he said, 'Our requirement is of CTVs with wired remote – not cordless as some customers pilfered the remote unit when they checked out of the rooms. Dyanora wanted a time of 7 working days to come out with their proposal.' The market for a wired remote did not exist! I told Mr Khanna, 'Allow me 5 working days instead and I would check and confirm if Solidaire could provide a prototype.' Mr Khanna replied that if we could, the order for the 100 TV sets would be ours on the same terms. I had won the initial battle and thanked Deepak to have introduced me to the GM.

Next was a working day as usual, as the city administration had been able to control the situation considerably. I narrated the previous day's incident sounding, Ravi Prakash, Ramana Prasad (the elder brother) and Anoop Kumar and asked whether they could provide a prototype of a TV with a wired remote in 4 working days. Anoop was quick in decision making (and that's why small companies flourish even today). He spoke to Pranab Basu and gave him directions on how it could be done.

The prototype was delivered to me on the 4th day, and I, along with Pranab, carried it to Mr Khanna. The concept was successfully demonstrated. Khanna shook my hands, returned to his office, and handed over the purchase order of 100 CTVs. Rest became history. A chain of events followed as Solidaire was the first to introduce the concept of a CTV with a wired remote that would eliminate pilferage. Our next order was from Hotel Ramada Inn for 200 CTVs.

I did not keep a track of what followed as by mid-March, 1988, I had decided to leave the company to re-join Philips India. But whenever I got to meet the Chairman of the company or the two directors Ravi and Ramana Prasad at the airport, they invariably said, 'We miss you in our good times.' By that time Solidaire had gone public.

Key Learning:

How much are we willing to sacrifice? We must be committed to doing the best job, even taking personal risks at times. The hunger to win any game allows us to transform every negative into a positive. When the entire city was in a disturbed state, it was an obstacle yet an opportunity too. Yes, luck also matters to a great extent. But when desired results are not achieved, we often attribute it to bad luck, and when something positive happens we attribute it to our hard work. It is often said that luck is something we can create for ourselves and learn to control, which means we can teach ourselves to get luckier – making tweaks to the way we approach opportunities that arise in our daily life. We live in a world where every single choice we make has consequences.

Many people do not pay attention to little things that may have an enormous impact.

When rivals would be in their homes, hiding gave us the impetus to push our product. It is amazing how receptive a buyer could be when there is chaos outside and we two were the only friendly faces he had seen all day.

Vignettes from My Diary

My lighting division counterpart while at Philips India R. Vasudevan found out the PWD in Tamil Nadu was about to invite tenders for the supply of a huge number of single fluorescent light fittings. The Superintendent Engineer, known to him, phoned and asked if Philips had a ready stock of this item since their requirement was rather urgent. Vasudevan knew that even if he quoted the commercial price at a special discount, Philips would not be able to match the competition offers which would be way below. He rushed to meet the Supt. Engineer and offered to supply the fluorescent lamps, ballasts, starters, and lamp holders on D G S & D Rate Contract and send the samples. by the fastest mode of transportation.

Since the PWD was eligible to place orders on Rate Contract, Vasudevan was able to persuade the Supt Engineer to issue a Rate Contract order, obviating the need for him to issue an open tender where our chances would have been nil to bag the order.

20

The Pied Piper of Sadar Bazaar

The Pied Piper of Hamelin is a classic story of yore. The German town of Hamelin was infested by rats. It became a big problem. Dressed in a 'pied' (multicoloured, primarily black and white clothing in the middle age) outfit, a piper offered the mayor of the town a solution to their problems in return for a promised sum of money. However, the mayor refused to pay the money once all the rats were driven out into the river alleging that he brought the rats to the city himself. Enraged and vowing to take revenge the piper played the pipe – he played the flute once more when all the adults were in the church. The children of the city followed him, and they walked into the river never to return.

Once, some years ago, my friend Mr Pawan Kapur who was invited to deliver a guest lecture to my students, narrated a story that always reminds me of the Pied Piper. Pawan had started his career with the Shriram Group of Companies (founded by Lala Shriram) as a Management Trainee. At that time, it was one of the most prestigious entry-level jobs for a graduate/postgraduate in any field from well-known universities. The company had launched a plastic tricycle in 1976 made from HDP (High-Density Polypropylene) named 'Tobu' in Delhi and he was assigned the responsibility of selling and creating a market for this cycle. He appointed a distributor at Old Delhi's Sadar Bazaar – a wholesale market where everything a shopper or a retailer can dream of was available. The introductory price of the tricycle was Rs.150/- as opposed to Rs.60/- of the conventional metal tricycle popular those days. But Tobu cycle was far superior in aesthetics, design, child-safety (round edged), convenience, and being very child-friendly as well as it was a sturdy yet much lighter in weight toy. Unfortunately, however, sales were not taking off. My friend decided to visit Sadar Bazaar market to understand the ground realities and the reason why the product was failing in the market.

As usual, the distributor whom he had appointed grumbled about the pricing – customers who were used to paying Rs.60/- for a metal cycle would never consider buying a Tobu at that high price. His retailers were hesitant in placing their indents. The distributor's retailers were scattered around Connaught Place, Karol Bagh and in the rest of the Delhi and New Delhi area. He took considerable effort in explaining to the distributor why a customer should prefer the Tobu to the metal tricycles, but it did not impress the distributor. Exasperated, my friend finally borrowed a Tobu cycle and requested one of the salesmen to take him around Sadar Bazaar market and introduce him to the retailers who sold tricycles.

Carrying the tricycle in one hand, my friend started meeting the retailers as he walked around in the lanes of the crowded market. At one shop while he was explaining the features of Tobu, two small kids were curiously looking at the tricycle as they were seeing it for the first time. Slowly they came forward and touched it and smiled at each other. My friend asked, 'Would you like to sit on it and take a ride?' The kids nodded their heads and taking turns, both the kids rode the cycle for a couple of meters in Karol Bagh's congested market. They requested my friend for more rounds. They were visibly thrilled. The retailer watched on. Slowly some more children gathered there and each one wanted a ride.

The retailer offered to accept two Tobu tricycles and my friend had got his first order then.

What followed was the story of the Pied Piper as the young sales executive proceeded to meet the next retailer. By then, about six children had joined the procession. All of them took their rides one after another. Another two pieces of the order were acquired from the next retailer. He went on visiting retailer after retailer with a group of children enthusiastically following him. And halfway in between the number of children had swelled to make a motley group, quarrelling amongst themselves to take the rides. The enthusiasm of these kids was quite overwhelming. When my friend was ready to leave the market, twenty-odd kids were still excitedly waiting for their turn. My friend turned into a real Pied Piper of Delhi!

He had a confirmed order for 60 Tobu tricycles. In return, the distributor signed an indent for 75 more Tobu cycles for immediate delivery. It was just a day's hard work of a salesman as a foot soldier.

This story was repeated elsewhere in the country and became a successful brand.

Key Learning:

When someone focuses solely on selling a product based on its pricing, not understanding its unique selling proposition, it is always difficult to sell. Add to it a salesperson's lack of physical presence in the market. When the product concept is new, the concept must be sold first to sell the product. Selling should be on value and not on price. Whether it is a children's tricycle or a thermal power plant makes little difference.

In creative selling, the salesperson goes out to create a need or unravel an existing need. When a crowd gathers around the salesperson it gives him/her a chance to sell the merchandise. Today, the sales job is becoming more and more creative because it is extremely competitive especially with the conflict between online and offline. The salesperson must be alerted to find new opportunities, new territories, new channels. When nothing works, it becomes the sales manager's task to become a 'foot soldier', working shoulder to shoulder with the sales team to be able to demonstrate, create a desire and finally get a customer to place an order. My friend was successful because he persisted and demonstrated resilience in handling rejection.

(With inputs from Pawan Kapur)

21

Think Strategy, Choose Change

On a cold winter evening in 1972, Mr Nanda of Radio Service Company, the top Sales & Service dealer in Himachal, drove down to my house in Delhi in a jeep. His face showed that he was in great hurry; he wanted me to accompany him to Shimla where the dealer was based. Unable to sell the newly introduced Philips Audio product, due to a technical glitch, he was saddled with a large quantity of stock. He needed someone from the company to find a solution to the problem. Prior permission for my visit to Shimla had already been taken from the Regional Service Manager. As a service engineer, who at that time was heading the workshop at the Janpath office in New Delhi, I packed my bag as fast as I could and drove non-stop to Shimla, halting mid-way for dinner, only to reach our destination much after midnight. A decent set-up had been pre-arranged for my stay at a newly constructed hotel. The next day, I repaired the defective sets, as many as I could in their small workshop, and guided his son Narinder so that he could complete the rest. Our relationship was founded from that day onwards and even as I write this book, Narinder and I remain in touch. There have been similar incidents during my tenure, as I was promoted to the position of Regional

Service Manager. It led me to gradually develop a deep bonding with the dealer fraternity in the Northern region. The Naini train accident described in one of the stories *(No. 12)* is a case in point.

I was not so successful in maintaining a similar attachment when I was transferred to Madras (now Chennai) in early 1981. A devastating cyclone had ravaged Tamil Nadu (TN) and Coastal Andhra in November 1980. It brought in miseries, which had not been seen for many years, and caused significant damage to the infrastructure as well as caused mass destruction to the habitation. I was to take over as the Consumer Electronics (CE) Sales Manager for the Southern Region. My predecessor had a very good track record, with a performance that was well-recognised. On the face of it, I needed to only adapt myself to the new role to keep the wheel moving. Unfortunately, the transfer was timed in the midst of the cyclonic destruction. Tamil Nadu had, all along, witnessed a sales growth of the highest level among all the states in the region that comprised Andhra Pradesh (AP), Karnataka (Kar) and Kerala. The Southern Region was ranked number one in CE sales for several years in succession. The sudden jolt in Tamil Nadu's contribution, due to the cyclone, made a major dent in the overall CE sales of the region. For me, getting a grip on the situation required time. The southern states were quite different culturally and the cities were less cosmopolitan compared to now. The language barrier was another impediment. Even after six months down the line, my struggle had not ended. To offset the loss of sales, I concentrated more on Kar and parts of AP that remained unaffected by the cyclone.

Business in Kerala was vastly different. Remittances from overseas Keralites, who worked in the Gulf countries, contributed to around 20% of the state GDP, thereby giving consumers a good buying power. Despite this, Kerala's contribution to Philips' sales figures was the least amongst the four states for the reason that the company had very little control over the sales. For historical reasons, Kerala was being serviced by two large distributors, whereas Philips, as a matter of a national policy, was sold only through dealers unless they were located in the hilly districts of North East India.

The two distributors in South Kerala and North Kerala were SK Enterprises and NK Enterprises, henceforth SK and NK, respectively. They sold over their own counters and through a network of sub-dealers that they had established themselves. Amongst them were several very large outlets and we were not allowed to contact them on our own; we had to be accompanied by SK and NK. Order booking, sales discussions and everything else that mattered had to take place with these two distributors, who imposed only their own terms. Aside from this, the distributors ramped up their margins to cover for their distribution cost. It made products much costlier than the prevailing prices in the neighbouring states of TN and Kar; this resulted in more market share loss.

The way forward, for us, was to correct the existing anomaly in the dealership network. Thus, we strategiz ed to make direct appointments to the Kerala market, in the territory under the control of SK and NK, in main towns as well as in the hinterland. We thought of further expanding the network by making new appointments in underrepresented markets. It always intrigued me that why did my predecessors allow the status quo to be maintained? Perhaps they were in their comfort zones and so were unwilling to disturb the set-up or their relationships, while things overall were going good.

The then Regional Manager (head of the Southern Region) was a senior with whom I had worked in the Northern Region and I did not need to convince him of our strategy. He gave his approval and asked us to proceed carefully. I also received full support from the Sales Executive based at Kerala. Our plan was to make a joint visit to each and every outlet of SK and NK without keeping them informed; we would talk to the retail outlets, understand their problems, and offer a right product mix and promotional support (which until now was in the domain of SK and NK). Along with my sales executive we travelled across the hinterland of Kerala. It took 40 days to assess how many of the largest dealers of SK and NK were willing to be associated with Philips directly. SK and NK were distributors of other consumer brands as well, which further placed them in an advantageous position. This provided the retail outlets (sub-dealers) a single contact point for their entire consumer product requirement, including Philips. Despite this hindrance the responses were overwhelming. We were further convinced that direct dealership would result in a significant increase in the company's sales, both in the short and the long term.

Following our visit, we met up with SK and NK at their respective offices. We discussed our future product plans and that the range in the consumer electronics arena would impose severe financial restrictions. The business partner of SK dismissed our suggestion. He maintained that on the one hand, the company was unable to supply the fast-moving products while on the other we were insisting that they increase sales by promoting the higher priced models. Competition from foreign brands (mainly National), he said, brought into the state by the Gulf workers, was disturbing the market. When no compromise seemed forthcoming, terming that it was working against the company's interest, SK threatened that if Philips made direct supplies to any outlet in 'their' territory, SK would surrender all their sub-dealers at one stroke; and we would be exposed to arrange for service and logistics support. Whereas talking to SK did not help, the business partner of NK, appreciating the rationale behind our move, was forthcoming and agreed to cooperate with the new terms of arrangement. NK would ask all their big dealers to directly buy from Philips in Chennai. NK's support went on to the extent of supporting us in the interim with logistics backing, in case SK's threat was to become a reality.

Consequent to our visit, two letters of SK's sub-dealers, one from Chenganur (in Kollam district) and another from Pathanam thi tta were on my desk. I found them upon reaching the office. The letters alleged that it was becoming problematic dealing with SK. They expressed their keenness to forge a direct relationship with Philips even if that meant defying SK. Cheques were enclosed for fresh supplies mainly consisting of the higher priced models. The matter was referred to the Regional Manager for approval of the two direct appointments. With the tacit support of NK, these supplies were made.

After a week, a letter was received which read: '...*You have planted a cancer cell inside my territory. If status quo ante is not revoked, you may take over the complete responsibility of South Kerala territory from me by appointing your own set of new dealers. You may take into your fold all my sub-dealers, only if you are able to convince them to take your direct dealership – signed . . . Business partner SK Enterprises*'

Having worked on the field and having understood the ground realities, the threat was ignored. Following this action, the two distributors' roles were reduced to selling our products from their own showrooms only. The process to streamline the operations took a couple of months. During the initial adjustment period, NK provided us the required support to overcome the teething problems.

I had just begun to settle down with the role and was becoming acquainted with the market when my transfer to Mumbai was announced for a newly created support function. Two years into the sales function was noticeably short unless there was a hurrying need to get me over to Head Office. Was it the outcome of our strategy? Were we too brash in the execution of our decision or was the mission accomplished? The answer has always eluded me.

Fast Forward:

A breakthrough had been reached in Kerala with sales increase reflecting in the overall performance. I had gone to Chennai for work after six months of the transfer. My successor revealed that the business partner of SK had a visibly bruised ego. Seemingly, he started keeping an indifferent attitude. The SK showrooms continue to flourish even today.

The Regional Manager too retired from Philips shortly after I moved to Mumbai.

Key Learning:

Strategy means making hard choices. Sometimes it is a trade-off between competing for market shares and maintaining a relationship. Relationships matter in life as well as in the workplace, but to be able to strategize, you may need to decide on one way or the other. Change must be accepted with grace. The organisation benefitted from my effort to streamline its operations. But the other party was unable to accept change. Sometimes people are required to do and accept unpleasant things to get better results.

22

What's So Special About Nordstrom

If 'clothes maketh a man,' then perhaps shoes make or break the entire look. A pair of shoes truly mirrors the personality of a man. Though I am impartial to style, I value a good pair of shoes for reasons like comfort, durability, and affordability. The brand or the look of the shoes come a close fourth.

On my visit to the United States in the recent past, my hunt for a *Heritage* collection of a New Balance pair of walking sneakers that carries the tag '*Made in America, Worn by the World*' ended up with a pleasant experience. In the beginning, though I would come across New Balance shoes that were all made in China. My persistent search took me to an upscale department store chain Nordstrom at the Stanford Shopping Centre in the Bay Area of Northern California where I located the product.

Four years prior to my shoe hunt, I had read about New Balance shoes as a lead story in *Time* magazine. It was an interesting article on how New Balance continued to succeed despite stiff competition from popular brands like Nike, Reebok, and Adidas in the United States. The 1.5-billion-dollar Boston-based New Balance Athletic Shoe Inc, globally recognized as a leading manufacturer of high-performance athletic footwear and apparel, had prided in American roots since the year 1900 and sold its products in more than 120 countries including India. The company focused on improving technology and production methods and it was the only athletic products company that still manufactured footwear in the United States. The cover story prompted me to ask my son in the United States to get me a pair of this brand of shoes, more out of curiosity, but also as it suited my daily walking habits. He got a pair that was made in China, like most things 'American' these days. One could hardly distinguish the newly acquired shoes from similarly priced sneakers that I usually wore except the name of the brand. My interest in the *'real'* American New Balance *Heritage* collection became more intense.

While looking at the different New Balance athletic shoes displayed at Nordstrom's footwear sale counters and curiously perusing the 'Made in USA' label I was greeted by a cheerful-looking young salesman who was curious to know what I was looking for. Most of the shoes carried the China tag with prices ranging from $60 upwards to $95. My search ended when he picked up a shoe displayed at the same counter that carried the US-made tag – and one that was of the *Heritage* collections. As I was looking at the shoes from all corners, he removed a tiny piece of price tag sticker that had got stuck on my jacket, glanced at it as $99 and smiled at me. (Believing the price of the pair to be $99, I imagined the price to be equivalent to INR 4800/- and decided that the pair was a steal considering the shoes were of US origin). He confirmed my foot size as US 7 and left for the storeroom to locate a suitable pair. In the meanwhile, as I was looking at the other ranges displayed, a smart-looking walking shoe of a different brand with a price tag of $75 drew my attention.

He returned expressing regret that my size was not available and the only one in stock was one size larger. Nevertheless, he asked me to try it out. Confident that it would provide a comfortable fit, he explained while measuring the size of my foot once again that he had noticed though my foot size was US 7, the ankle size was a shade larger and as a result, US size 8 would provide a superior cushioning effect to my ankle. I took a few steps after wearing the pair and though it left a gap between my toes and the far end of the shoe, walking was wonderfully comfortable. I silently questioned the wisdom of spending $99 for an oversized pair of walking shoes! The salesperson was observant when I asked him to show me the smart-looking shoe priced at $75 that had grabbed my attention in the meanwhile. After a while, he returned with a pair of my size (US 7) of this second pair which I wore and took a few steps. The comfort level of the New Balance shoe was distinctly superior. The conflict in my mind had disappeared; the decision had been taken to buy the New Balance pair of shoes and I enquired the final price. The salesman said $139 plus local tax which would make it around $152! A little while ago the price was $ 99 how could this pair be different?

He cheerfully said 'Sir, the $99 sticker was not of the Nordstrom store but of some other store that might have got accidentally stuck on your shirt'. I was in no frame of mind to spend INR 7500/-, the equivalent of $150 and almost prepared to leave the store. I casually asked him, 'I understand Macy's (another famous US chain of departmental store) was not charging sales tax to foreign visitors to the stores, so is there any possibility of waiving the tax since I am a foreigner here?'

The young salesman retreated, saying, 'I will find out just now,' and on his return after consulting a senior colleague revealed that Macy's scheme was not applicable at Nordstrom, though tax could be waived provided it was ordered online. But the transportation charges to India would itself cost $50, he added. By this time, the salesman had spent almost three-quarters of an hour with me.

The salesman subsequently suggested a few other quality brands of walking shoes in the price range of $65- $95 at their footwear counter and asked me to put them on. He also explained why the smart-looking pair I had tried was not suitable for daily walking. 'It doesn't offer a cushioning effect and is good for dressing up on a relaxed Sunday afternoon,' he said. He also took pain to elaborate why I find the size 8 New Balance I chose more comfortable than the other brands I tried – it supports my ankle, unlike others. Without appearing very persuasive he said, 'Size 7 of the same pair would be too tight for you. You actually need size 7 ½ , but that wouldn't provide much toe space like you get in size 8.' I admitted to myself that none of these shoes, though of the right size was as comfortable as the size 8 New Balance was. As I took time to decide, for the price indeed was high for a pair of shoes, the sales chap patiently waited on me, exchanging views, and bringing to me whatever pair I wanted to try. Finally, I decided to buy the pair for $152 and took out my debit card for making the payment.

It was clearly a bad day for us. For some strange reason, my debit and credit cards were all getting declined as soon as they were swiped. The salesperson then switched on to the manual mode to accept the credit card payment which was not the usual practice witnessed in the United States where persons manning the cash counters were very procedure bound. Finally, I got my first 'Made in USA' New Balance shoes!

What made me splurge to buy the pair of walking shoes that evening two times the price of similar shoes? Was it just it carried the 'Made in USA' tag? During our overseas visit, we are prone to mentally do an arithmetical calculation on how much it would cost us in equivalent rupees and whether it was worth spending the money when similar products were available in our country. This cautiousness was justified because my generation of

Indians was not brought up in a consumer society. I admit I had been influenced a great deal by that article in the Time magazine, and the more products with the 'Made in China' tag I saw, the more exasperated I had become, but I also realized that this was not the only factor behind that purchase.

Indeed, my experience at the store was a lesson in sales management. There are two main requirements for a successful business – a thumping good idea and a really enthusiastic sales force to go out and sell. My experience with the salesperson at Nordstrom was one of how to sell more effectively, satisfying customers, presenting the product and gain a commitment to buy. The salesperson later gave his visiting card that said 'expert shoe fitter'

Key Learning:

Salespeople don't sell. They find out what people want by focusing on customer's needs This helps to steer the customer to the 'finishing line'.

Skilled salespersons always try to generate trust by answering questions honestly. They do not make up stories just to motivate one to buy. He speaks with the best interest of the customer in mind finding out about those needs first. Buying signals can save a lot of effort if read correctly and close a sale in a seemingly natural way through the best mix of technique, timing, composure, and body language.

Salespersons learn about products, not in isolation, but one product in comparison with others in the range. They ought to know when to talk and when to listen to the customers – and manage to achieve a balance between the two.

23

How Not to Sell!

During the period of liberalization, a host of multinational companies were entering the Indian soil in the consumer electronics space tying up as joint ventures with Indian conglomerates. I did a short Business Development consulting assignment with one such company a well-known global brand. The Managing Director of the company was an overseas gentleman and new to this region. The market was dominated by BPL, Onida, Videocon and a host of regional players like Crown, Weston, Dyanora and Solidaire. It was a crowded and highly competitive market.

This company commenced its operations making its presence felt in all metro and non-metro towns setting up their branch offices headed by a Branch Manager. The Managing Director (MD) after a brief period announced a limited period sales promotion scheme for the dealers.

It said, *'A dealer who purchased more than 100 CTVs from 15th. May to 14th. June 1990 would be eligible to an expense-paid 7 days trip to the overseas parent company, and sight-seeing at exotic places in Japan.'* Standard payment terms were maintained ie 15 days from the date of billing. The tour was scheduled for July-August that year. It was expected that within this period the company would be able to sell 'X' number of CTVs providing the much-needed breakthrough. The company's product quality and reliability were distinctly superior. What lacked was the push from the dealers' counters.

Towards motivating the Branch Managers, the MD extended the scheme of the overseas visit to those who completed their targets. This created enthusiasm amongst many of them, others were sceptical. The Hyderabad Branch went overboard and got 24 dealers to be billed for 100 CTVs. Time to take the flight was fast approaching but payments were not forthcoming. In the first week of July, the MD while checking the status from the Branch Managers discovered that 80 per cent of the dealers of the Hyderabad Branch had not paid up. Other Branches managed to collect post-dated cheques with the hope by the time they returned the money would get credited to the company's account. The MD repeatedly questioned the Hyderabad Branch Manager, and his typical reply was, *'Do not worry Sir, payment will certainly come in before we leave.'* The MD trusted him and gave clearance to the defaulting dealers to undertake the overseas trip. There were 100 qualifiers including the Branch Managers. Many of them were setting their foot outside India for the first time. There was excitement. The MD, too, accompanied them. After a lot of bonhomie, fun and frolic, all of them returned to their homes with gifts for their family and duty-free liquor bottles. For the Branch Managers, it was an opportunity to get to know their dealers well.

Upon return, the MD looked at the accounts; most of the dealers had paid up albeit late, but 20 of the 24 Hyderabad dealers had not paid up at all or their cheques were dishonoured. No improvement in the status was seen even after a week of their return. The MD got enraged and in exasperation, ordered the Hyderabad Branch Manager to call back the CTVs from dealers' showrooms. When the TVs entered the warehouse most of them were irreparably damaged, others returned in used condition making them unsalable. Not only was the loss suffered by the company huge, but also one of belying trust. The Hyderabad Branch Manager was admonished by the MD and fired.

At a sales meeting held subsequently at their Head Office where I was also an invitee, the MD visibly annoyed started the meeting narrating the sorrowful incident *'We dispatched the TVs to the Hyderabad dealers at our expense, they kept it at their showroom for 3 months, even used them at their friends or relatives. They went abroad at our expense, yet never paid up. We had to cart them back to the warehouse at our expense. I have not experienced this anywhere in the world. This is not sales, when you do not collect the money, it is giving 'donations.'*

Key Learning:

Often quoted by Dr Len Rogers in Strategic Marketing course 'A Sales Policy is a Suicidal Policy'. The underlying meaning reflects in this story. Several new entrants in the market have made a good initial beginning and vanished all of a sudden. The trade is smart; they know manipulative techniques. The right course of action ought to have been a sales target with a corresponding collection target.

24

The Magical Return on Investment

….. A Backbone of Successful Business

By Atanu Gangoly

Decades ago, I was on my sales training in Varanasi. I was new to the FMCG (Fast Moving Consumer Goods) industry and was struggling with terms like distribution, coverage, primary, secondary, closing stock and that fiery word ROI (Return on Investment).

To an unsuspecting, finance shy bong, ROI was always an enigma. Until one hot summer afternoon, when a friendly, almost illiterate (loving and respectable for sure) distributor from an upcountry UP town asked me 'Hello sir, where are you from?' After exchanging sweet nothings, we started engaging ourselves in our respective businesses at the Carry & Freight Agent warehouse. I overheard a small conversation between him and the depot manager which attracted my attention.

'You have to take X cartons of Detergent if you want Y cartons of Vanaspati-main line, the Sales Officer has instructed me,' was the hushed but firm reply of the depot manager to some inaudible request of the distributor. Suddenly being aware of my eavesdropping, the depot manager smiled and said, 'I need to use these opportunities to push some sales, Sir.'

'Please yourself,' would be my answer now, cynical that I've become over years. My young mind, however, sensed something tricky if not extra-official. Innocently I asked what was the matter? Here came the stunning reply and my first encounter with ROI in practice: The said distributor was an upcountry guy who was enjoying what was known as 'Cheque facility' by the Unilever system in those days. They were known as Redistribution Stockists. While the company used to get the cheque discounted, the

Redistribution Stockist used to pay the cheque after any time between 7 to 14 days. So many of the Redistribution Stockists used to self-lift the goods and sell them on the way back at a discount and use the cash for trading into other quick rotation items such as spices, vegetables, and tobacco. This would stretch the money and get him a much better ROI than what it would usually fetch by just distributing HUL products.

Later, I discovered many such financial wizards sitting in our wholesale *mandis* who would sell everything at a rate 2% lower than the prevailing market price and make good margin loss and maybe much more from the sale of empty cartons. One distributor in a remote upcountry market explained to me how he calculated rotation of his capital every week thereby giving him a whopping 50 per cent plus ROI per annum.

Much later in life, when I was responsible for not just sales but also of profit and loss, I realised that the backbone of a successful business was above all a healthy ROI.

Key Learning

While selling is an art, it also is about commerce, and the bottom line of any business is a healthy Return on Investment. A merchant wholesaler turns his/her capital six to nine times a year at the cost of unit profit. Large organisations are unable to rotate their capital as swiftly as their intermediaries do as they do not have price flexibilities. At the heart of any business is the management of current assets – Inventory management (stocks) and debtors (bills receivables) – the key control factors for success. Aside from this, a salesperson must be dissuaded from the practice of selling by 'any means.'

Part Four

MARKETING & BRANDING

Marketing is all about creating demand. Branding or Brand is important not only for companies but also for customers.

A BRAND is an identification symbol of ownership. A marketing brand can be a symbol, a mark, logo, name, word, and/or sentence that companies use to distinguish their company or product from others. A combination of these elements can also be used to create a *brand identity*. Examples of brands are Microsoft, Coca-Cola, Ferrari, Apple, and Facebook.

Brand positioning is the conceptual place established in the target consumer's mind, the benefits of which are linked with a brand. An effective brand positioning strategy will maximise the relevance of the product to the customer and its competitive distinctiveness. Thus, brand positioning is how a product is differentiated from those of the competitors and how consumers identify and connect with a brand.

Brand positioning can be achieved by a variety of means including visual design, tone and voice, and the way a company represents itself in person and on social media. The positioning of a brand helps to inform consumers why they should choose it over competitors' product and is one of the few things that can be completely owned.

Your brand is reinforced by customers' overall perception of your business. Your brand is your reputation! A successful brand must be consistent in communication and experience, across many applications:

- Environment (shop front or office)
- Print media, packaging.

- Online publicity and website.
- Content publishing
- Customer service
- Employees' communications

Building a brand is a long-term process that requires a strategy that establishes long-term relationships with customers. Branding leads to a steady increase in leads and sales, word-of-mouth referrals and advocacy for your products or services. Your brand is defined by a customer's overall perception of your business.

Managing a brand is to create an emotional connection between products, companies and their customers and constituents. Brand managers may try to control the image of the brand. Ultimately a brand is something that resides in the minds of consumers.

(With inputs from Dr Len Rogers)

25

Where A Distributor Becomes A Brand

How many of us associate all photocopier machines with Xerox? Or a sticking tape as a Scotch Tape? There are examples galore when a brand name becomes the generic name for a product. The power of brands cannot be overstressed. And often an entire business comes to be associated with a brand.

In 2018, I happened to meet a gentleman in a major city in Lucknow, Uttar Pradesh. He looked after his family business that dealt with a large company that manufactured and marketed air conditioners. This gentleman, in his early 40s, dealt with this company as its distributor and was solely responsible for sales, installation and providing with maintenance/servicing of that brand of air conditioners. The business had grown over two generations, and they became the largest distributor of that brand in the city.

Over time the family's sincerity, focus on building trust, and delivery of consistent and quality service established credibility with the customers. They were responsible for making the company's products the #1 brand in the city. However, a change of company policies made the air conditioners manufacturers decide to end the system of selling through distributors and, accordingly, they intimated this young man's father who was still in charge. The young man, who was confident of his own hard work and the trust and credibility he enjoyed in the city, shot back to the company, 'You take over my business, and I am going to deal with another brand of air conditioners!'

He had learnt what made a brand popular and trustworthy and was confident that with the help of his bonding with his customers, he would continue to serve his customers well. Outside a retail sale where brand names matter, it is of little consequence in the business-to-business customer segment where complex installations are involved if the entity is the organisation or its channel partner. This distributor's image, developed over a long period of time, was irreplaceable which would enable them to take up any other competing air conditioners business and make it the top-selling brand. The family was known by their own name and was quite famous in the city. The air conditioners company was not prepared to topple the apple cart in a situation where the existing system was consistently profitable. Behind the power of the brand lied the sincerity and hard work of the family of service providers.

Key Learning:

A brand gets created by building strong customer loyalty. A customer values honest and open dialogue, product expertise, understanding of the needs and issues, what the product would do for them, responsibility across the supply chain, a high level of specialized expertise and their value and belief. If done correctly it leads to the channel partner's own identity becoming stronger than the brand itself.

A branded fast-food franchise in each marketplace can create its own base of loyal customers. If the franchisee decides to terminate the contract, the same franchisee can take up any other fast-food brand and their sales will not get affected.

26

A Peep into Rural India

Today, most management professionals know what 'rural marketing' is. It constitutes the heart of India and comprises a big chunk of any business. Two-thirds of our people live in our villages who contribute to 50 per cent of the country's GDP. During my times we needed to acquire first-hand knowledge for developing our market in the rural segment. My exposure happened quite early in life when I travelled to the Auraiya district in Uttar Pradesh in 1973 along with a Philips Sales Executive to meet a Philips dealer.

We met the dealer at his shop and after discussions took place, he extended an invitation for dinner at their house. Accordingly, we reached his house in the evening. He was, like many traditional Indians, very hospitable and made us feel comfortable. He then introduced us to his wife. We were seated in cosy chairs placed beside a 'charpai' where our host himself was sitting. As we conversed his wife served us dinner – vegetable dishes and 'daal' preparations laced with pure homemade ghee. It was in a 'thaali' and placed on it was a small bowl of ghee. 'Phulkas' came straight from the oven with a coating of ghee. Those were the days when we were not cautious about high cholesterol or unwanted weight gain. Hence, the taste of that food was divine!

At one corner of the living room, we noticed a buffalo. The dealer explained that the bovine creature was a part of their family and remained there throughout the night. That was the first time that I experienced rural India's consumer insights.

Choosing and positioning a product for the rural market is one of the most important decisions for a marketer. A study in this respect tells us how we are perceived in the mind of a customer. The following story that I heard at a Rural Marketing Seminar proved how the perception of a brand differed according to the profile of the customer.

Hair fall was a common problem in both urban and rural segments. Rural women were as aspirational as their urban sisters were, and thick lustrous hair appealed to everybody. Multinational companies had introduced several brands of hair tonic or shampoo that sold well in the urban markets. However, for a village woman, spending money on a branded hair fall shampoo or tonic would be considered as 'splurging' and would be viewed as extravagance amongst the family members. Therefore, an international personal grooming company repositioned the same product that sold well in urban markets changing its image as an ayurvedic product tinkered with the formulation but did not alter the price. It was a successful selling proposition from the beginning!

Connecting with a rural customer is a challenge that companies must overcome. During the 2007-08 Global financial crisis, the travel and tourism industry everywhere was severely affected. Big names like

Thomas Cook were no exception. It had already positioned itself as a company that offered luxury travel. It could not find enough customers from Maharashtra for an Italian summer holiday. I heard another interesting narration at the same Rural Marketing Seminar. Though big Travel and Tourism companies like Thomas Cook didn't find any taker for their Italian Holiday Package, the famous St. Mark's Square in Venice where tourists fed pigeons (now banned), large gatherings of Indian tourists were spotted the same year. Most of them were traders from interior Maharashtra. Their tour operator was a home-grown agent Kesri Travels. Kesri Travels probably had charged the same amount as Thomas Cook did, but the perception of the customers was different. While Thomas Cook offered 'luxury holidaying' as their positioning, Kesri Travels promoted the holiday package as a 'stress buster'!

Same product, the Italian Holidays had two different types of consumers.

Another time, another place. I travelled with a colleague to Ratlam city in Madhya Pradesh, visiting a Usha Sewing School. These schools were Usha International's initiative to empower the village women, developing a special skill. It would enable many to become entrepreneurs by opening independent tailoring shops or by teaching sewing to more women within the village community at a later stage. It also resulted in more sales for Usha sewing machines. Once trained, the learners would start buying and the brand Usha would be more ingrained in customer's mind and result in increased sales.

Several village women had enrolled in the classes. However, one strange discovery was made – young women who turned up to the school early would first head towards the washroom. Coming to school dressed demurely in salwar-kurta, their normal village attire, these girls would first change into jeans and top. This was to be their first step towards emancipation and self-assertion!

Positioning of the brand is as important in a rural set up as it is in urban markets.

Key Learning:

Tools, approaches, and strategies have to be deployed carefully by organizations to successfully build their brand in the rural markets. Branding is managing expectations. With media exposure and increasing literacy levels, people in rural India are demanding a better lifestyle. To be successful, we must understand

- *The buyer*
- *The product*
- *It's positioning*
- *Branding*

Due attention has to be paid to the psychographic aspect ie lifestyle, self-concept, self-values (goals for life) while positioning and the right pitch.

27

Birth of A Brand

By Ashish Sen

My first stint in HUL (Hindustan Unilever) was in its commodity business, far removed from its FMCG segment. From 1986 to 1992, I was with a small team of managers running its brand-new Fertiliser business headquartered in Kolkata, selling DAP (Di-Ammonium Phosphate) manufactured in Haldia. It was a business compelled by the 'Core-Sector' involvement that all multinational organisations had to comply within the pre-liberalisation era and one that was totally alien to Unilever anywhere, worldwide. And yet, I was lucky to be part of a marketing success story that was the envy of even HUL's FMCG businesses and their marketing whiz-kids!

Indian Fertilisers comprised the following, besides some (Potassic) nutrient Muriate-of-Potash:

a. SSP (Single Super Phosphate) with 18% Phosphatic (P) Nutrient Content.
b. Urea with 46 % Nitrogenous (N) Nutrient Content; and
c. DAP with 64% (18% N + 46% P) Complex Nutrient Content.

Fertilisers were 'completely regulated' essential commodities those days. The Government decided who produced the fertilisers and how much was to be sold in each state for an easier reading and was sold 100 per cent through 'registered' (licensed) fertiliser dealers, at uniform and inflexible prices across India. Each fertiliser, whosoever was the manufacturer, had the same chemical (molecular) composition and same nutrients, also the same mandated packaging. These controls, normalising availability across states as per consumption, were to protect farmers ensuring exactly the same quality, quantity, and price.

Retention pricing and freight subsidies further normalised business results to similar levels, reimbursing under-recovered costs due to the enforced 'control price' of sale, and granting similar return on investment for all – with little regard for efficiency or inefficiency. HUL's returns, despite superior technology, people, and practices were frustratingly like even a sloppy industry. Though in fertilisers for core-sector compulsions, HUL felt the industry's eventual decontrol was inevitable.

The first step towards this was choosing a new technology reducing plant cost by 25 per cent – a capital efficiency enabling great competitive edge once decontrolled. Step two was building a premium brand and becoming both the trade and farming community's choice, despite a control regime.

In the beginning, HUL launched its 'PARAS' DAP in 1987 and was allotted market-territory covering West Bengal, Bihar and the North-Eastern states – all with multiple pre-existing DAP players. Fertiliser brand names were little beyond logos on bags with regulatory printing and bags across brands looked quite alike, filled with the print matter on rather drab backgrounds. Beyond filling-quantity norms, the law allowed for handling losses, prescribing minimum fertiliser quantity in bags at point of sale. Into this hardcore commodity market entered HUL with the vision to make PARAS DAP the No.1 choice across markets using their fresh entry and enabling processes for brand-building unheard of in the industry.

Then the paradigm shifted. From being a standardised commodity to a Preferred Brand HUL took 2 years to establish itself in the market. These were the days when branded FMCG platforms themselves found consumer choices shifting from sheer brand recall and preference to product properties spelt out on packages; like Total Fatty Matter (TFM) in the personal wash or Active Detergent (AD) in fabric wash categories. Yet, here was HUL attempting just the reverse in fertilisers – of moving a sheer commodity to a brand.

HUL adopted a 4-pronged strategy of tested initiatives to move away from the industry's commodity trappings and drive PARAS DAP to a compelling brand leadership by marketing the category's core strengths appropriating them into the brand story. The company's DAP was the most superior fertiliser type with the highest nutrient content. From now on a focused and sustained reiteration of the strengths was built into all brand communication both written and verbal.

To ensure high visibility and brand affinity with consumers, a bright yellow bag with attractive lettering and logo in bright green and red was created to be an eye-catcher that paled out the rest. It was also much stronger, with far higher specs than what industry used, or laws required. HUL spent 15% above the bag-cost allowed for subsidies under Retention Pricing. This withstood transit rigours much better, and remarkably helped preserve the quality and quantity of contents. Its attractive looks and strength also opened many reuse opportunities in rural markets like cycle-rickshaw hoods, sheds, or carry bags etc. The resale value commanded a higher price – sometimes even higher than HUL's cost for fresh bags. It soon became a rage, almost a status symbol among farmers across markets.

HUL unleashed an intensive advertising driveway beyond any past industry effort, dotting roads, towns, and villages across markets with attractive wall paintings – effective, relatively inexpensive but high visibility advertising with proven rural marketing success in HUL's other product lines.

PARAS DAP's awareness and recall value soon exceeded any marketer's dream – not just as top-of-mind but also as top choice both among farmers and the trade. In a staid commodity market, HUL offered a never-before product promise by assuring customers of bag replacement if even 1 gram was found short in their 50 kg bags. For this, HUL not just used better bags as above, but in their plant, they also installed the most sophisticated and accurate bagging system worldwide at a huge cost. While few bags really needed replacement, PARAS and HUL gained popularity with farmers for fair play and reliability.

Perhaps in a first for the industry, HUL created a salesforce entirely of Agri-scientists – mostly first-timers, moulded into tech-savvy, much sought after 'friends of farmers.' Their managers, proven professionals in rural sales from other HUL businesses, hand-held their selling skills development while a senior scientist from Manila was hired as the technical mentor. He honed the Agri-science understanding and application skills of the team, creating a crack team of professionals fraternised and respected by both the trade and farmers. A slew of other outreach programs like year-round question and answer programmes through postal and radio transmission, regular farm visits, Kisan melas and training sessions further reinforced the PARAS team as true friends of farmers. In just 1 year, PARAS DAP entrenched itself across markets as a true partner to the Agri-community.

PARAS' runaway success and brand leadership were evident by the second year. It became the first choice of farmers and traders and the first DAP to sell out. With laws prohibiting premium pricing, HUL successfully 'pre-sold' PARAS well before sowing season (when DAP was required), collecting sales proceeds months in advance.

This amazing market leadership was further reinforced after DAP's decontrol in 1992. Despite the withdrawal of subsidies causing an uproar and increasing prices by 100 per cent over earlier 'control prices', PARAS commanded 10 per cent price-premium over other DAPs.

The birth and brand-building of PARAS is truly a tale of cutting-edge marketing – remarkable branding of a pure commodity into a differentiated and highly preferred product!

28

The Big Launch of a Small Car

by Debashis Paul

One of the powerful stories drawn from my marketing experience in my rather fat treasure-house is about the launch of Hyundai Motor Company in India and the Hyundai Santro, in 1998 – often regarded as the most successful car launch in the Indian automotive industry by CEOs, marketing professionals and by industry-watchers of the day. It's a success story that is built around many proverbial 'firsts.'

BROAD STRATEGY

In the wake of the liberalised policies of the Indian Government in the early 90s, there had been a transformative effect on the automobile industry (particularly in the passenger car segment). However, none of the new global players, namely, Fiat, Ford, GM, Daewoo which had entered the market with the mid-size Sedan offerings could pose any real threat to the deeply entrenched Indo-Japan giant – Maruti-Suzuki. Their awe-inspiring market share stood rock solid at about 80 per cent at that time.

Hyundai leadership took an entry strategy decision that was different from all other global players – to enter India with a small car. The segments size accounted for nearly 60 per cent of the market and the might of Maruti-Suzuki in the segment had hitherto made it a no-go zone for new international players. Hyundai decided to enter by fighting the hardest battle first – with a view to build consumer confidence that could be leveraged for long-term play.

- Produce a small car with 60%-75% indigenous manufacturing for better cost-management and thus competitive end-pricing.
- Build capacity for sedans and other mid-sized cars to follow the first launch in subsequent years to establish a wide range.
- A strong national distribution strategy and dealer training program to handle tier-1 and tier-2 towns across India.
- Service centres that would set the highest standards of customer experience quickly on-field (many global players had left a lot to be desired in this department in India).

The first-generation Hyundai Santro was revealed in early January 1998, in the India Auto Expo held in Pragati Maidan in Delhi to the accompaniment of the classic Korean drum orchestra. Saatchi & Saatchi, India had won the 10-agency competitive pitch and showcasing the car at the Expo was the first task to handle.

Two weeks before the event, I was asked to move to Delhi from Calcutta, (now Kolkata) to take charge of the Saatchi & Saatchi office as Vice President & General Manager and to primarily focus on the gigantic new account. The

Corporate and Marketing office of Hyundai, for various strategic reasons, would be functioning from Delhi with close liaison with the manufacturing facility and HO in Tamil Nadu.

MARKETING STRATEGY

- To develop a marketing strategy for the launch, a thorough research was conducted across many chosen cities.
- In the final customer evaluation in the research (technically, called the Car Clinics) using conventional criteria, there appeared to be some gaps in comparison with Maruti Zen, the then leader.
- Santro was slated for launch pre-Diwali that year in the backdrop of steep competition.
- An out-of-the-box marketing communication strategy had to be developed if Santro had to gain early success. Needless to add, the titanic force of Maruti-Suzuki on the ground had to be pushed back.

The broad communication strategy in a nutshell:

1. Register the name Hyundai in people's minds as a tech car company and multi-area businesses with a successful track record.
2. Lay the 'success markers' of Hyundai by way of a 'corporate campaign' but with a difference – in the first phase (3 months)
3. The second phase of the campaign plan on the primary medium TV was to raise the curiosity level of the Indian customer about Santro – its features and the new value additions to the city. In other words, insert new value equations in buying a small car.

4. There were tactical advertisements planned in print media to showcase direct comparisons with competitors that were to come – this was a 'first' in the passenger car category advertising in India.

The question that was central now was the creative strategy.

We were exploring a brand ambassador led campaign to carry a credible message to the Indian customer who would be filled with scepticism. All the reservations about a Korean auto player (which did not have the traction of Japanese/European/American names) had to be allayed. Quick research was conducted to map the image – attributes of public figures/celebrity given the challenges on hand.

- It is important to note that no automobile brand had used a celebrity or a public figure, in brand advertising until then in India. So clearly this would be a 'first.'
- After careful evaluations by the agency team the recommendations were placed to Hyundai that popular Bollywood actor Shah Rukh Khan should be brought in as brand ambassador owing to his massive appeal in the middle-class families and his 'believable' next-door boy image.
- The South Korean automaker had never used a celebrity in advertising anywhere in the world, it was indeed a big, strategic call that the top management had to take.
- After we got the decision to go ahead the creative teams across Saatchi India offices got down to work round the clock.

THE POSITIONING & ITS EXECUTION

- The marketing insight was taken into consideration that in the Indian middle-class psyche the family was central to many of the middle-class values.
- The symbolic value of upward movement and individual achievement in society were anchored in the emotion-laden notion of 'my family.'
- The care and convenience of women, the elderlies at home – easy to park advantages that mattered for women drivers were also considered.
- The feeling of space in a small car to carry day-to-day things in a typical family and the involvement of the family members in the buying decision were other driving factors.

That was then the rationale for the family-centric strategic positioning of Hyundai Santro. In sum, be it the functional values or performance values of the car or the emotional values, they needed to be hinged on the canvas of 'my family'.

The second phase of the campaign carried the signature: Hyundai Santro – The Complete Family Car.

- A light-hearted narrative approach with Shah Rukh Khan being persuaded by the South Korean Hyundai manager was the basic construct and the advertising tonality would be non-preachy with a note of humour and a strong sense of the real.
- Shah Rukh Khan would pose the questions rather crisply and candidly to the Korean Manager, the questions, and doubts of the sceptical middle-class car buyer – starting with how exactly the name Hyundai should be pronounced to why is the high-tech MPFI engine better? And why the 'tall boy' design?

Also, the scripting would allow Shah Rukh's experimental, fun persona to rub off onto the Santro brand thus widening its appeal amongst all age groups and lending a youthful aura to the brand.

Many years later, I worked with Shah Rukh again at my next agency McCann Erickson Advertising on various other brands – in our banter in the side-lines we used to reminisce about those early years of his endorsement career – Santro, he used to say, was one of his landmark assignments and had remained a favourite till then.

My hands-on learning of how to use a top-notch brand endorser for maximising mileage proved to be of immense value in my later career with a plethora of global and Indian brands.

The Saatchi stalwarts at the time – Shanta Kumar (Managing Director), 'Bugs' Bhargava Krishna (National Creative Director) and Shubhabrata Ghosh (Strategy Director) led the creation of the national campaign.

THE LAUNCH OUTCOME

- The campaign started 4 months prior to the official launch date with bookings open.
- The media strategy was impeccably executed to ensure consistency over those 4 months and deliver high impact.

- On the launch day in October 1998, the register shot up to 15470 fully paid bookings (the target for the launch phase was 7500 cars. So more than 100 per cent of the results against the booking objective was accomplished on day one!
- A consistent rising pattern of sales followed in January 1999.
- In July 1999, sales overtook Maruti – Suzuki's Zen (1000cc) the chief competitor in the price band that Santro was operating in.
- Brand track studies in the top 12 cities of India showed a top-of-mind awareness of 70-80 per cent post ad campaigns and brand imaging showed that Hyundai was a 'friendly, consumer-oriented company, dynamic in its approach.'
- Santro was rated as the 'Best Car' in its segment in an opinion survey among all makes of car-users in Delhi, historically, the largest car market in India!
- In the next 2 years, Santro clocked a healthy annual sale of 60,000 cars.

Then came a series of updates that helped the brand keep up its image of 'new tech'-

- The Santro Xing with a bigger and boxy stance with a revised front and rear design.
- CNG variant with dual fuel options around 2007

The Santro franchise helped build the foundation of Hyundai Motor Corporation in India and it quickly emerged as the second-largest player with a wide range of passenger cars on offer and the brand grew from strength to strength. The Hyundai belief in good advertising to build a strong consumer connect and long-term brand equity has played a crucial role in delivering success over the last 2 decades.

THE MAGNIFICENT COMEBACK

Hyundai India brought back the Santro moniker in 2018 as the entry-level hatchback segment was lying vacant! This was to be a momentous occasion for all of us associated with giving birth to the Santro brand. Naturally, it fills us all with a sense of glory to this day. We – all the talents of the Saatchi India team and the Hyundai Marketing team – got together to achieve it.

In the year following the first launch, we won the trophy 'Winner of the best advertising campaign' in the world in the category of Auto Consumer Vehicles. It was the Advertising Marketing Effectiveness International Awards 1999 organised by New York Festivals. Several big wins had followed, just to name a couple of them: Gowtam Ghoshal Trophy from the Calcutta Advertising Club and the Best campaign of the Year Gold from the A&M magazine.

Let me end with the observation of Mr S S Kim, MD & CEO, Hyundai Motor India Ltd, on the World Car of the Year Awards 2019 –

'We are extremely delighted and proud with All-New Santro's nomination in the 2019 World Urban Car category – World Car of the Year Awards (WCOTY). The All-New Santro is a true expression of Hyundai's technology and design prowess for Make in India for the World. Since its first launch in 1998, Santro created history with its numerous segment-first innovations and became the Complete Family Car for millions of Indians.'

Part Five

TECHNOLOGY IN BUSINESS

Technology is relentless. Industry 4.0 embraces Artificial Intelligence, Machine Learning, Cloud Computing, Big Data/ Analytics, Mobile Internet, 3D Printing, Cyber-Physical Systems, Robotics, Augmented Reality, Internet of Things (IoT) and Advanced Materials. Disruptions, technological or otherwise, continue to alter the business model of a large number of industries – transportation, hospitality, health care diagnostic, insurance, customer service etc. Now, all of a sudden another disruption – the global outbreak of Covid-19 has altered the overall perspective and has posed big questions on the economic front, manufacturing, business models, future of jobs and many others.

Companies rely on technology because it wants to:

- Increase revenue
- Provide greater customer satisfaction
- Create a highly-skilled workforce
- Make business process agile
- Develop a growth mindset
- Improve decision making
- Provide better quality products
- Add greater brand value

Artificial intelligence (AI) is having a bigger impact on the world than some of the most important innovations in history. One evening I realised how AI could be a game-changer in business and customer experience in all the fields. I would order medicines online every month on a certain day of the week because the online portal would offer a 20%-25% discount that day. I routinely kept an hour aside on that day of the last week of every month for this job and would enjoy the discount for medicines of my family. But like all successful start-ups, this online pharmacy was acquired by a business house soon and I realised that the discount on the medicines had ceased to be offered. Instead, I would receive messages from this online portal, now owned by a different name in the healthcare industry, offering schemes/discount in a random fashion. I shifted loyalty to my neighbourhood shop that offered me only a 10% discount and delivered my medicines at my doorsteps. This is where AI would have helped the new company in charge of the online medicine delivery portal retain old customers like me. Since they do offer discount schemes but on random days, they could use AI and customise the offers a bit. If I received a message of the discounted rates a day after the 20th or 25th of each month, I would not have looked for other choices. Similarly, AI could reveal the buying habits of other loyal customers too and help the new owners in the business. It would have benefitted both the business house as well as the customers.

As customers migrate from offline to online for all their necessities, the big winners are the companies with online presence. Extending the analogy to retail buying experience let us say a brick-and-mortar retail outlet having an online presence (omnichannel capabilities) ie if you make a purchase online on their website in the morning and then go into their store in the afternoon would the staff there know about the product you had bought a few hours earlier on their website? And if, in the following morning you phone the retailer, would they be aware of your purchase and your last store visit? If they are, that would truly be a seamless connected customer journey.

With the proliferation of mobile connectivity and usage, the ultimate experience will be for customers to walk into a store with their mobile phones and the store recognises when they last used your services. The customer opts into the brand via their phone, which tells them there is an item they might want that will be coming in-store in 2 weeks time and if they would like to be one of the first people to buy it. And that is happening instantaneously.

29

Think Design

Design Thinking is the latest high impact business tool of this decade. It is the confluence of all management aspects from human resource to time management to leadership, leading to increased productivity, better performance, and higher employee engagement of any business establishment.

A people-centric approach where professionals look at how people work and then following a few simple steps that the *Design Thinking* process involves, reach a universally accepted solution to improve working in an organisation. There is no hi-tech theory and requires a lot of involvement of all the departments of an organisation for breaking new ground. And it produces amazing result!

Steps to be followed:

1. **Listen, Observe & Take Note**: In a bottom-up method, the Design Thinking team of professionals observe and get talking to everybody taking part in the day-to-day activity of an organisation. They take note of the slightest gesture of inconvenience/unhappiness of all the stakeholders of the business, including the customers.

2. **Empathise and Understand the User**: In this respect, the management should be able to understand sympathetically the emotional state of the stakeholders who use the work procedure established in the system. It includes even the temporary and the contract workers and also the customers – paying attention to customers' expectation is as important as not losing focus of the business establishment's own interest and emotions.

3. **Define the Problem Area** – Spending time in the business establishment the *Design Thinking* team gathers insights into the process and working of the people involved, how professionals and unskilled employees do their job, how they interact with one another and respond to crises or sudden demands of their superiors including how they use technology. This step is important to deliberate later the problem areas to enhance productivity at all levels.

4. **Ideate**- Through brainstorming with parties involved, looking for a solution to address the specific problems, new ideas are generated. The process involves noting down experiences and points of view of everybody involved to get a broader view of the problem which help arrive at possible solutions. Here leadership of the organisation assumes an important role – no scope of personal ego here, and no sense of superiority should impede the outcome of the brainstorming sessions.

5. **Prototype**- In the next step after reaching solutions with the help of all the stakeholders, the focus is

shifted on one model out of many workable solutions.

6. **Test** the efficiency of the model by giving it to the user, and watch how they use it, the time spent on it and what software is used. The result often is much more rewarding than one can think. Optimisation of time and workload is the key to the successful implementation of the solution and increase productivity and efficiency of the organisation.

Health Care, the most important of all services industry can benefit from Design Thinking. I had been hospitalised recently, at the very beginning of the long lockdown period in 2020. It was for the same ailment that had demanded medical intervention many years ago. I contacted the same doctor of the private hospital who had treated me in the past, and he asked me to come to the hospital in an emergency as all hospital OPD working had been suspended temporarily. A junior doctor was expecting me at the emergency, and the senior doctor who had treated me earlier had already briefed him about the course of treatment. I needed to be admitted, and here appeared the first stumbling block that negated the efficiency and productivity of the system. The admission procedure was long, and it can be rather exasperating for the family who would be attending to the patient – even during the apparent lull of lockdown when there were not many patients waiting, the procedure took almost 45 minutes, keeping me wondering whether anything was amiss in my medical files/insurance papers or the credit card payment procedure.

Later, post-discharge, I was required to contact the doctor/hospital for a follow-up. I had to go through an online appointment process, and in my own interest I consulted the doctor – again it was through a video call as it was amidst an extended lockdown period. Expenses for private hospital treatment is prohibitive even after possessing a medical insurance plan. As a patient it would have made so much of a difference to me had there been a follow up call from the hospital/doctor's office since I had paid a handsome amount for my treatment.

When something is missing, this is where *Design Thinking* steps in to help in a major way. In private health care, it improves delivery and productivity by identifying blind spots in the process or the software engineering team. Kaiser Permanente, a leading US-based health care provider organisation has adopted a human-centred design methodology that involves health care professionals and patients as collaborators in the innovation process. And in this way, apart from providing a better health care system, the organisation is discovering more intangible benefits like a happy employee and greater patient satisfaction. Better delivery of health care services post-hospital discharge has been achieved at Kaiser Permanente through a care coordinator who can step in between a specialist Doctor's valuable time and a patient's peace of mind. A similar presence of a care coordinator in any hospital can reduce the numbers of continuous phone calls that a doctor receives during his consultancy time with a patient. This is just an example. The ambit of *Design Thinking* is all-encompassing.

Design Thinking has been gaining popularity because of its people-centric approach. Since the service industry is all about people and since the emotions of both customers and company employees play a major role in deciding the success or failure of the business, *Design Thinking* can help increase the efficiency and productivity of the service provider.

To cite a few examples during the Covid 19 outbreak, adopting Design Thinking techniques State Bank of India became #1 in Mutual Funds crossing Rs.4 lac crores. Eureka Forbes commenced Digital Demonstration & Digital Service. From a village in UP, a salesperson sold 16 Vacuum Cleaners to a customer in Mumbai. MV Augusta had not sold a single unit of their motorbikes in the last 3 months, sprang up with a surprise to launch the Warrior UV Disinfectant that kills 99.5% viruses & bacteria. They contemplate partnering with Eureka Forbes for direct selling of the product. WFH that was limited to technology, the scenario has leapfrogged enabling Godrej Housing to sell flats on WhatsApp. Adani Group enhanced the process of touchless check-in at airports and employed AI & Face Recognition Technology. Designers can add a lot to the strategy and process of change management.

The current global pandemic has led to a lot of innovative thinking and problem-solving at multiple levels in organizations.

30

Towards E-Commerce Strategy

By Upal Chakraborty

E-commerce is slowly but surely overtaking traditional brick-and-mortar commerce. The COVID situation has only accelerated the speed of this journey.

Unfortunately, the strategic approach is generally lacking in the e-commerce segment. The focus seemingly is to replace brick-and-mortar selling without opening the floodgates to fresh perspectives and vistas. The expectation of the customer today is not just for the vendor to drop the merchandise at his doorstep but provide him superior levels of services and act as a source of knowledge not provided hitherto. Customer Service needs a paradigm shift for its positioning as a source of revenue enabled by technology.

I have tried here to provide a strategy for e-commerce in today's competitive environment.

The Concept.

Position the e-commerce platform to provide adequate levels of Customer Service in the form of knowledge, suggest alternatives, satisfy his queries instantly and adequately on products and services available, the status of existing deliveries, prices, discounts, etc. The unique profile of each customer needs to be derived to be able to predict his proclivities and tailor products and services to suit his identity.

The Multiple Possibilities.

- AI (Artificial Intelligence) for Customer Service will not only make self-service interfaces more intuitive and economical but assist in anticipating specific customer needs from their contexts and provide proactive knowledge. This will be enabled by the creation of customer profiles based on a dynamic criterion.
- Create a knowledge base to provide adequate levels of Customer Service to satisfy his queries instantly and adequately on products and services offered, the status of existing deliveries, prices, discounts, etc.
- Proactively, with the help of Artificial Intelligence and Analytics, assess his profile and from similar contexts derive the probable likes and dislikes to suggest products and services which could be of interest.
- Employ the services of an advanced Chatbot so that most queries are catered to automatically. Control will be transferred to the Customer Service Executive only if it is not able to respond to the queries. If not available, CSE will call back later. For non-savvy customers, telephonic support will continue to be offered but armed with information from the database. The knowledge base will be enhanced with every interaction. When CSE is interacting online with the customer, the Chatbot

should be automatically updated. When he speaks on the phone, he will manually update after the conversation. Thus, the Chatbot becomes more and more intelligent and knowledgeable as days go by.

- Define customer behaviour patterns through AI-powered analysis combined with Data Analytics.
- Proactively track the movement of goods and inform the customer if there is a delay or a hiccup, predicting possible arrival times.
- Vendors must also be provided feedback on their pending deliveries, customer feedback, etc. and predict their sales daily for them to stock adequate inventories.
- An AI-powered report shall be generated to highlight customer issues, assess satisfaction levels through Natural Language Processing and their behaviour on the cart. This will act as a competitive advantage since most customers do not enjoy filling feedback forms.
- Provide a superior and seamless purchase experience to the customer and sort out issues based on live and virtual interactions.
- Attempt to capture his contexts – if ordering food for a party, on a holiday, a marriage ceremony, official meets, etc. There should be a special focus to capture bulk orders and ensure that orders are repeated.
- Proactively identify customers with the potential to place food orders in bulk for social ceremonies or official meets like off-site meetings. Software

should proactively identify such individuals and incentivise them.
- Allow customer superior navigation using the drill-down approach.
- Superior integration with social media – Facebook, LinkedIn, YouTube
- Explore social media to determine current trends and products buzzing among customers and determine locational/ethnic preferences.

To exemplify, a customer orders chicken regularly through an aggregator for non-vegetarian food. He orders boneless chicken and chicken keema but lacks the time to explore the site, thus missing the announcement that they have started serving chicken roast and semi-cooked chicken kababs recently. Also, let us assume that Punjabis prefer the kabab whereas Bengalis generally prefer the roast. It is the job of the software to discover whether chances are high that the customer who has logged in would opt for the kabab or the roast. This is impossible in retail outlets of the traditional format. Analytics will help to determine the correlation between ethnicity and the choice made, and thus suggest one of the two to the customer. The moment a Bengali person logs in, it should inform him of the availability of the roast. No point in informing him of the entire range of new products on offer, since most find it irritating to view a cluttered screen. It may be that there is zero correlation between preferences for the chicken roast and ethnic identity and instead, there is a high correlation on the age group – the younger generation freaks for the roast. So, it will suggest the roast when a young person logs in.

It will also create a repository of information from past customer orders to provide relevant information. For example, a Punjabi gentleman in Kolkata with no knowledge of Parsee food has invited a few Parsee guests. A night before, he gets a brainwave to treat them to at least one original Parsee dish. He should be able to rely on the software to educate him on the best options available in Kolkata – based on past purchases of others like him.

No premium food-delivery app today attempts to create a profile of the individual from his characteristics and behaviour and purchasing history. Not much information is asked for, and options limited to a listing of joints nearby and the deals offered. There is no attempt to discover what suits the customer by recognising him as a unique individual.

How to Differentiate the Customer?

Three methods of differentiation are generally followed- psychographic/lifestyle approach, consumer typology approach, and demographic approach.

- The psychographic/lifestyle approach categorises customers based on shared psychological characteristics like beliefs, motivations, psychological makeup, etc – in other words, his patterns of thinking and feeling. These are normally unearthed through structured questionnaires, but administering questionnaires is tough and involves an expenditure of both time and money and therefore it is imperative to capture behaviour patterns from the online behaviour of the customer.

For example, loyal customers who have stuck for a long time and progressively increased sales may form a category, like impulsive customers who purchase at random – maybe a biriyani today and a sweetmeat tomorrow. Maybe other, need-based customers who purchase above a certain quantity – presumably when there is a party at home – form another category. Value-oriented customers who search for value and not price form another category and finally there is the cost-oriented customer.

- The demographic approach is most widely used, based on demographic profiles like age, gender, ethnic identity, religion, location, etc.
- The consumer typology approach to classifying customers based neither on psychographic makeup nor demographic variables but unexplained or positively irrational behavioural characteristics. For example, a customer is in the habit of abandoning his cart midway or orders an item in the 1st week of a month or late at night. Most of these are not based on rational criteria but random behavioural characteristics.

A statistical correlation must be determined between demographic characteristics/consumer typo/psychographic category and purchasing behaviour of the groups based on the characteristics described above. Purchasing behaviour may be products or experiences, frequency of purchase, values of products purchased. This will help in proactively suggesting the right products at the right time and new products and experiences (cross/upselling) to the customer based on the profile he belongs to. The amenability of various categories of customers to promotions and deals could also be determined in real-time. High-value customers can be offered deals and preferential treatments as soon as he logs in or be communicated through messages and emails.

Strategizing the approach to e-commerce is critical today. The one who does it first and the best will always have the first-mover's advantage. We have witnessed Trump's electoral success through Cambridge Analytica. It is now time to utilise the capabilities of Analytics and Artificial Intelligence for business.

31

Mid-Life Crisis in Tech Jobs

By Punya Palit

The 'National Employability Report for Engineers 2019' put out by a job assessment platform Aspiring Minds, has shown that over 80 per cent of engineers in India are unfit to take up any job in the knowledge economy.

Let us analyse the root cause of this serious problem.

In the early days of Information technology (the Mainframe era), only large organisations could afford to employ IT staffs. They used to hire engineers from reputed engineering colleges and trained them in-house on a specific technology. Computer Science as an undergraduate subject was not available and hiring was done primarily based on aptitude and specific interest. Many of these engineers eventually left for lucrative overseas jobs and I belong to that generation. Unlike my peers, I came back to India after spending 15+ years abroad and started my new innings here. Most of my colleagues predicted that I would not be able to settle and would be back within six months, but I proved them wrong.

In the year 2000, there was a new India. Programming courses were available in every nook and corner and most of the engineering colleges were offering Computer Science degree at the undergraduate level. The trend was to do a certification in Java or similar technology, and you will get a passport to go to the USA, the land of opportunities.

During my tenure with Microsoft, I visited many engineering colleges for campus hiring and got a chance to speak to many aspiring engineers. This was how the conversation went with most of them.

Do you enjoy coding?

'No. Not at all.'

Then why did you waste 4 years to do a computer science degree?

'This is the only way you can get a job these days.'

But if you do not enjoy programming, how can you keep your job?

'I will survive two to three years and then move into management.'

I was puzzled as this was the common reply, I received from most of the aspiring engineers in 2000. With Y2K, there were more opportunities for the engineers to go overseas.

Then I changed my job to IBM Global Services, where we needed to hire many IT professionals (mostly engineers) every year. I took note of the culture and thought process of most of the Indian IT services company.

- Programming was a low-end job. It was meant only for freshers or less experienced resources.

- In the western world, you would still find a fifty-year-old programmer writing code, but it was unthinkable in India.
- If you were experienced and still writing code, it meant you were a loser.
- The only way to progress was to put a managerial title in front of your name.
- The easiest way to get that was by doing a PMP certification (internationally recognised professional recognition offered by the Project Management Institution).
- Indians somehow mastered the art of passing the certifications by studying the dumps i.e., memorising past questions and answers.
- Once you became a project manager, it was beneath your dignity to do programming. It was meant for junior folks or those who could not be a manager. Someone correctly said 'it was beyond their capability' once they reach this level.

As a result, today, if you take a sample of the population from the middle management, they are totally hands-off and are only involved in administrative functions. They survive only because of their relationship and active participation in company politics and totally away from the ground reality. When the onsite/offshore model first started, there was a huge margin and organisations could employ many of these managers in non-billable roles. But over the year with steep competition, these managers will find it extremely difficult to keep their job. Most of the IT services companies will have very few non-billable positions going forward.

Once the middle-managers lose their jobs, they become unemployable.

In Australia, I found a 40-year-old person enrolled for an undergraduate degree course at night. When I asked him why he had taken such a late decision in life, his reply was, 'I am not doing this course to get another job, but it is going to help me to do my current job better.'

In India, the majority of us study to get a job and not because we like the subject. But what happens when you are not able to cope with the emerging trends and do not have an aptitude for the subject you have studied?

It is better to struggle in the beginning and getting it right. When you are in your forties, you have financial commitments and losing your job at that stage will be catastrophic for the entire family.

That is the story of the middle managers in the IT industry today. A few years ago, the problem started when you were in your fifties and with recent generations, it will start much before. So, one must prepare oneself for all kind of eventualities. Learning continuously and keeping up to date with the changing trends is the key.

If I look back over thirty years, I was part of the Head Office Technical Support team for NEC Australia. We used to support different branches in Australia and New Zealand which supported more than four hundred customer installations. This was the era of computer hardware and three of us were called 'Astra Gods' by our colleagues. There was no cell phone those days and my desk phone used to constantly ring every day and we were providing different answers and solutions to the customers and branch support engineers. Occasionally we needed to visit customer sites to solve a specific problem. But we would have simulated the scenario in our lab and already found an answer to the problem so that we could spend minimum time at the customer premise. Though we were at the bottom of the pyramid, we used to get tremendous respect from the sales leadership and management team.

So, the mantra for survival is 'Stay current, stay relevant, learn continuously and Enjoy the Journey.' Does it sound right? Are you hands-on and hands-off?

Part Six

MY STORY

Education

From standing first amongst the candidates of my school (Sardar Patel Vidyalaya, New Delhi) in the 1961 Higher Secondary Board Examination to winning the best faculty award at the New Delhi based Business School in 2019 is the story of my long journey from corporate to management education.

1966: BITS, Pilani   *1969: IIT-B*

1964: BITS Fest
College orchestra playing the
harmonica (1st. from right)

1967: IIT-B With famous
singer late Geeta Dutt
(front row 1st. from left)

Philips India Ltd. New Delhi 1969- 1980

Joined Philips India as a Management Trainee after completion of M. Tech from IIT- Bombay in 1969. Out of the 19 years I spent in the company, the first decade was at the Regional Service Centre in New Delhi when I became the Regional Service Manager in 1976. With a string of good performances, the management transferred me to Chennai as Regional Product Sales Manager in 1980. I would consider this as the best period of my tenure. Learned about service management, human resource management, customer satisfaction and leadership. *(Story 1: One Champagne Bottle, Two Stories)*. My colleagues warmly nicknamed me *'Dadu'*.

L to R: Addressing dealers in a meeting, International Branch Service-In charge Training, Philips Convention, Secretary Philips Radio Dealer Association at farewell in 1980.

Philips India Ltd.
1980 – 1986

In 1980, I took over charge as Regional Product Sales Manager Consumer Electronics (South). This was my first exposure to product sales that provided me with opportunity to travel the length and breadth of South India and understand customers and markets. In 1983, I was transferred to Head office at Mumbai as Product & Market Support Manager where I continued till 1986. *(Story 21: Think Strategy, Choose Change).*

1982 Dealers' Meet Top second from left. With visitors from Head Office & Secretary PRDA (South) Bottom: Meeting with proprietor of Quilon Radio Service (front) and Sales Officer at Kollam, Kerala 1982 (Story 21)

Solidaire India, Chennai
1986- 1988

In 1986 I joined the Chennai based family managed # 1 TV brand, Solidaire India as General Manager. The experience here was vasty different. I assisted them with industrial design, making inroads into new markets, product launches and institutional orders *(Story 19: Opportunity Doesn't Wait)*. Learned about the art of collaboration and relationship in Selling and Marketing.

1986: New Market launch of Solidaire TVs, Kolkata with Mr. K Dutta (Branch Manager, left) and MD Mr. Ravi Prakash (right).

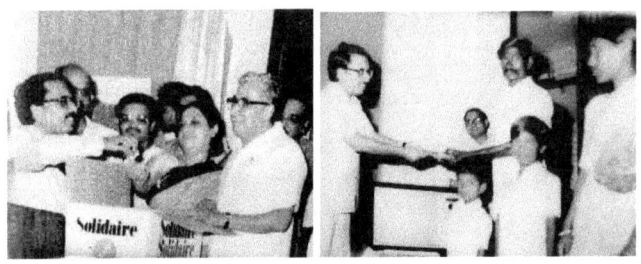

Lucky Draw Chairman Srinivasa Rao at Chennai (left), TV donation for a special cause at Trichy (right)

Philips India Ltd. 1988- 1990

I was recalled by Philips India in 1988 to head the Video Marketing Division at H.O in Mumbai in the Product & Market Support function. Left the company in April 1990. Learned about Product Management, Strategic Marketing, Branding and Advertising.

1989: All-India Video Marketing Conference at H.O. Mumbai

BPL Sanyo Utilities & Appliances 1990- 1994

1991: Launch of BPL-Sanyo washing machine, microwave oven and refrigerator at Nagpur

National Panasonic India 1994- 1996

Joined the Japanese multinational right from inception in 1994 at New Delhi Head Office. Panasonic CTVs and Audio systems were launched with a lot of expectations. Unable to face the onslaught from competitive brands the company decided to exit the Consumer Electronics field. At Gurugram they have since established a regional hub for the Asiatic, Middle Eastern and Western economies. In the two years I spent learned about Quality Management, Service Training and Customer Excellence. *(Story 14: His Fault, Their Fault, Not Mine)*

L to R: With Adachi San, GM Service, New Delhi, Clockwise from left: MD Shinozuka San (3rd. from left) and Japanese visitors, Daily Morning departmental meeting.

Usha International Ltd. 1996- 2007

Pictures of Annual Business Conventions

In 1996 I joined Usha International Ltd. as Senior General Manager of Appliances Sales and After Sales Service. The 4-day Annual Business Conventions an important event held at exotic hotels was attended by the H.O senior managers and Divisional heads where annual plans were presented. After 11 years in 2007 I left upon reaching superannuation age. Learned about Sales, Marketing, Operations, Enterprise Resource Planning.

IILM Institute of Higher Education, New Delhi, 2007- 2020

I had discovered the 'new me' while at Usha International, where a once-a-week I took up part-time management teaching at Bhartiya Vidya Bhavan. Subsequently, in 2007, I started working full time with IILM Institute as a Professor of Marketing and worked till the commencement of the pandemic in 2020. I continue to be associated with them as a visiting faculty. During this tenure, I have conducted Management Development Programs for PHD Chamber, CII, CICU, Daikin Airconditioning, Orient Electricals, Monte Carlo fashions and many other MSMEs.

Preparing Next Generation Managers

Comments of Past Students and Alumni:

- 'Your experiences are 'gold' and your story narration has always been a great learning. Thank you for providing your knowledge to all of us!'

- 'Sir has been a great teacher and a mentor as well. He guided us several times with his immense knowledge of industry and economy. His punctuality and sincerity never failed to inspire. I continue to look forward for advice and suggestions from him whenever needed.'

- 'We are fortunate enough to have a faculty like Sujit Sir to teach us the core lessons of sales and marketing. The lesson come very handy in day-to-day operations. Sir is the perfect blend of corporate experience and teaching experience. Only teacher who has lived through his case studies - (we) are lucky to be his students.'

- 'Really laud the effort to put together meaningful marketing and selling stories for posterity. Constantly, urging achievers and not-so achievers, to contribute can be quite a daunting task. But the single-minded sincerity to put together a visual aid for future students from Indian and International Business Schools is exemplary'.

Contributors

Dr Len Rogers was my Professor at Philips India. In 1968, Philips Gloelampenfabrieken NV, Eindhoven invited him to undertake consulting and training in marketing and finance around the world which continued until 1982. He is also a professor of management and finance at the International School of Management (Paris, New York, Shanghai, Tokyo) conducting research, tutoring mature students online and on-campus and supervising doctoral dissertations.

Ashish Sen is a Chartered Accountant who articled with PWC has 34 years of work experience with ICI, HUL and PepsiCo. From a grounding in Finance and business-analytics, he went on to senior leadership roles managing key inbound and outbound supply chain verticals in both HUL and PepsiCo at the national and corporate level. Mr Sen is an authority in several supply-chain management aspects across FMCG & especially Foods & Beverages (F&B) industries.

Atanu Ganguli is a Postgraduate in Economics with 34 years in FMCG Food and Beverage at various levels starting as a sales executive for famous soft drink brand rising from the positions of Area Manager to National Sales Director, Country Manager and Business Head of various brands eg, Unilever, Wrigley-Mars, Danon, Shaktibhog etc. Post-retirement he is dealing with two start-up ventures in the snacks and beverage category as Director.

Debashish Paul studied MBA from IISWBM, Calcutta, and graduated from St. Xavier's College, Calcutta, and has over 30 years of Industry experience. He was Executive Vice President & General Manager at McCann Erickson Worldwide. He was part of the win at New York Festivals - Best International Car launch campaign, and a part of the winning team of 2007 Cannes for Best TVC Silver Award for HappyDent. He is now a brand development consultant.

Gautam Sengupta is a B. Tech from IIT Kharagpur with over 35 years of industry experience in Products and Services businesses with functional expertise in Sales and Marketing. He worked with Philips, Unilever, Cadbury, GE, ABP and Zee Television.

Teaching Experience as Guest speaker at IIM C, IIM B, IMI, IIT Kanpur. Have taught full time for a semester in KCT Business School Coimbatore.

Oscar Braganza is an accredited CEO Coach, in the field of Technology, Media, Mining, FMCG, Manufacturing, Pharma, and Entrepreneurial spaces. After initial years in a career spanning Philips India and Usha International, Oscar has logged over 21 years of experience as CEO. From his first assignment in 1991, as CEO of Funskool, an MRF/Hasbro joint venture, Oscar has been CEO of a number of diverse companies.

Pawan Kapur is a Management Consultant and Strategic Advisor at JV International. After a successful tenure with Shriram Group of Industries where he started his career and launching Tobu Tri Cycles for children, he joined a British Multinational 'Roneo Vickers' looking after Sales and Manufacturing. Subsequently, he joined the British

Based Binatone Electronics as Director Sales and Marketing in India. Following this, he joined Panasonic India in its formative years as Vice President and later Bharti Enterprises as CEO of Bharti Teletech.

Prakash Waknis is an electronics engineer and worked in Philips for 31 years. After doing consultancy for some time, he joined Symbiosis Centre for Management and HRD. During his 15 years there, he acquired certifications – Certified Supply Chain Professional from APICS in 2007 and Project Management Professional from Project Management Institute 2011 – both US-based Institutions.

Punya Palit is a national scholarship holder and part of the second batch of Computer Science & Engineering graduates from IIT Kharagpur. After a decade of experience in the IT industry (India, Australia, USA, and Japan), a small stint in the field of academics, he is now associated with the Digital Marketing field. He has summarized his findings on Indian IT Industry and has given a message for the freshers and middle managers on career development.

Dr Tushar Roy is a heart specialist in private practice having completed his MBBS from Calcutta University, MD in Medicine from Delhi University and Post Doctorate DM in Cardiology from PGIMER Chandigarh, MRCP from the UK and a member of Royal College of Physicians of Edinburgh. He also completed law graduation and possesses a special interest in preventive cardiology & medicolegal aspects of medical practice. A voracious reader with a reading range from Prasna Upanishad & Zeno of Elea through Thucydides to quantum mechanics & artificial intelligence.

Upal Chakraborty After graduating from IIT (Kanpur) (MSc) and IIM (Bangalore), has spent around 35 years of working experience at various Corporates like Reckitt Benckiser, Pepsi, DLF, etc, the bulk as Head of IT/CIO at the Corporate level.

Yogesh Mathur Starting his career from the lowest cadre at Philips India Ltd. in a total span of 23 years with the company, he climbed from the position of Area Sales Representative to Regional Product Sales Manager finally reaching the level of Head of Sales and Marketing in the Head Office Consumer Electronics and appliances.

www.ingramcontent.com/pod-product-compliance
Lightning Source LLC
LaVergne TN
LVHW022013060526
838201LV00034B/340/J